FIVE IN A ROW

FIVE IN A ROW

Scotland at the 1990 World Cup

SHAREEF ABDALLAH

First published by Pitch Publishing, 2025

1

Pitch Publishing
9 Donnington Park,
85 Birdham Road,
Chichester, West Sussex,
PO20 7AJ
www.pitchpublishing.co.uk
info@pitchpublishing.co.uk

A CIP catalogue record is available for this book
from the British Library.

ISBN 978 1 83680 152 8

Typesetting and origination by Pitch Publishing

Printed and bound on FSC® certified paper in line with
our continuing commitment to ethical business practices,
sustainability and the environment.

Printed and bound in India by Replika Press Pvt. Ltd.

Contents

Introduction

FRIDAY, 13 JUNE 1986. Incredibly, having lost unluckily to Denmark and following a battling defeat to the powerful West Germans, Scotland were on the brink of making history.

Victory over reigning Copa América holders Uruguay at the Estadio Neza 86 in Nezahualcóyotl would send the Scots into the second round of the World Cup for the first time in history, as one of the best third-placed teams in the group round. As ever, the problem facing acting manager Alex Ferguson, who replaced Jock Stein after his tragic death in Cardiff in September 1985, was a lack of goals.

Going into the tournament Scotland had only scored seven goals in seven games. They had failed to score against East Germany at Hampden in a friendly and Australia away in the World Cup play-off second leg, and only won 1-0 in Israel in a January friendly.

An encouraging 3-0 win over Romania in March 1986, in a game to mark Kenny Dalglish's 100th appearance when he was presented with a special gold-plated cap by Germany legend Franz Beckenbauer – which is currently on display at the Scottish Football Museum at Hampden – raised the Tartan Army's spirits. Andy Goram started for the first time as a superb chip by Gordon Strachan, a fine Richard Gough drive and a late Roy Aitken strike were enough to see off the Gheorghe Hagi-inspired Romanians. They had missed out on the World Cup by just a single point, despite drawing with England home and away in qualifying Group 3.

On 23 April 1986, in an unusual spring fixture, Scotland faced the Auld Enemy at Wembley – St George's Day. A midweek game led to a lower crowd but 68,000 fans still packed into Wembley. The Scots were defending the Rous Cup, which they had won for the first time at Hampden in May 1985, after a Gough header secured a famous victory at a rain-soaked national stadium.

If the game finished level after 90 minutes, the trophy would be decided on penalties. Ferguson chose a strong side with Willie Miller and Alex McLeish in tandem after Alan Hansen had pulled out of the squad. This led Ferguson to drop the cultured Liverpool defender from his World Cup squad, as he later explained in his 2000 autobiography. With Jim Leighton injured, it would be a perfect chance for understudy Goram to stake a claim for Mexico. However, Ferguson opted for the experience of Alan Rough in his 53rd and final cap. The Hibs keeper was aiming for a record third win at Wembley, following a 2-1 victory in 1977 and a 1-0 success in 1981.

Scotland lined up as follows:

Rough
Gough–Miller–McLeish–Malpas
Nicol–Aitken–Souness (c)–Bannon
Nicholas (Nevin 56)–Speedie

It was a workmanlike midfield with the flair of Paul McStay, Jim Bett and Davie Cooper surprisingly left out.

Scotland began confidently, forcing a series of corners and free kicks, before they fell behind to a Terry Butcher header following a Glenn Hoddle free kick. Only a superb save by Peter Shilton from captain Souness denied Scotland an equaliser, but before half-time Hoddle headed a second goal after Rough had parried a powerful long-range shot by Kenny Sansom. Ferguson, assisted by Dundee United coach Walter Smith, chose not to bring on McStay or Bett and instead pushed right-back Richard Gough into midfield to support Charlie Nicholas and David Speedie. Steve Nicol moved to right-back and Aitken the right of midfield.

On 57 minutes Scotland were awarded a lifeline when, after exchanging passes with Gough, Nicholas was hacked down by Butcher. French referee Michel Vautrot awarded the penalty, although the England defender claimed that the offence was just outside the box. After a lengthy delay while Nicholas, who had damaged his shoulder, was replaced by winger Pat Nevin, Souness fired confidently past Shilton. Despite late pressure and a flurry of corners, Scotland could not find an equaliser and England held on to win 2-1. Ferguson claimed Scotland had not deserved to lose and bemoaned his side's bad luck. It was their first defeat in over a year, in a run stretching across eight games.

A few weeks later, a much-changed line-up, including a debut for Ally McCoist and a superb performance by Davie Cooper, earned an impressive goalless draw with the Netherlands in Eindhoven. In World Cup preparation, Scotland then acclimatised to the Mexican heat and altitude by beating LA Galaxy 3-0. They were later guests of honour at a Rod Stewart concert.

In their opening game of the finals they prepared to face a skilful Denmark side who had dazzled in qualifying and finished as semi-finalists at Euro 84. Notably, they had beaten England at Wembley to qualify for the finals in France.

On 4 June 1986, Scotland lined up at the Estadio Neza 86 as follows:

Leighton
Gough–Miller–McLeish–Nicol
Strachan (Bannon 74)–Aitken–Souness (c)–Malpas
Nicholas–Sturrock (McAvennie 61)

Maurice Malpas started on the left of midfield with Steve Nicol at left-back. Scotland began confidently and almost took the lead when Gough fired narrowly over, then Nicholas, looking sharp, had a shot blocked, before Michael Laudrup's runs troubled the Scotland defence. Willie Miller was in superb form but skipper Souness looked out of sorts.

Just after the break the Danes took the lead as striker Preben Elkjær fired in off the post after the ball broke kindly to him off Miller. Ferguson threw on Frank McAvennie, who went close with an overhead kick, and Dundee United winger Eammon Bannon. But Scotland could not find an equaliser and would finish the game with only ten men after Nicholas was brutally hacked down by Klaus Berggreen and had to be carried off, after the Scots had used both substitutes. A 1-0 defeat was harsh; Scotland had battled well in the hot conditions and deserved a draw. Aitken had fired home in the second half but the goal was wrongly ruled out for offside. Where was VAR when you needed it!

Alex Ferguson had raised eyebrows when he picked his World Cup squad. He left out Mo Johnston, his team's joint top scorer in qualifying, after his two goals sunk Euro

84 finalists Spain in a famous 3-1 win at Hampden in November 1984. Kenny Dalglish scored his 30th goal to equal Denis Law's scoring record, with a brilliant curling strike. Sadly, he had withdrawn after needing an operation, following Liverpool's FA Cup Final victory over Everton, which sealed the First Division and FA Cup double at Wembley.

Ferguson said he left out Johnston for his off-field antics, after Scotland had drawn 0-0 in Australia in December 1985, to become the last country to qualify for Mexico. Johnston later admitted to having a girl in his room, but claimed it had not affected his form. Ally McCoist, the SPL top scorer with 28 goals, was also left out, despite an impressive debut against the Netherlands. Steve Archibald replaced Dalglish, a surprise as he had not played regularly or even scored for Scotland since a header against New Zealand at the 1982 World Cup.

Paul Sturrock was also picked despite the fact that he had not played in any of the qualifiers. Graeme Sharp of Everton and West Ham's Frank McAvennie were the two in-form strikers in the English First Division. McAvennie's strike sealed a 2-0 win over Australia at Hampden, as the Scots won a play-off to qualify for their fourth World Cup in a row.

Charlie Nicholas, who had been on a good run of goals for Arsenal, was also included, but since his stunning debut goal against Switzerland in March 1983 he had been in and out of the side, mostly as a substitute. David Speedie was overlooked, which he bitterly complained about at the time, but Ferguson dismissed him as a moaner.

Next up in the so-called 'Group of Death' were Franz Beckenbauer and his powerful West Germany side. Assistant coach Craig Brown would later recall that German assistant Berti Vogts had told him he had spied on a Scotland training session by donning the T-shirt of a soft drink company at the side of the pitch.

Needing at least a point to keep Scotland's hopes of progress alive, Alex Ferguson put his thinking cap on and opted for a 4-5-1 formation. Steve Archibald was up front, as he was used to man-to-man marking while playing for Barcelona. David Narey came in for Alex McLeish who had gone down with a stomach bug. Gordon Strachan was given a free role as an attacking midfielder with a licence to get into the box.

Leighton
Gough–Miller–Narey–Malpas
Nicol (McAvennie 61)–Aitken–Souness (c)
Bannon (Cooper 74)-Strachan-Archibald

In the baking midday sun of Querétaro's Estadio La Corregidora, Scotland made a nervous start. The Germans hit the post and Jim Leighton made a fine save from a corner. Then against the run of play Strachan fired Scotland ahead; he famously put his leg only on an advertising board to celebrate. In the heat it was vital that the Scots held their advantage for as long as possible. However, within just five minutes Rudi Völler equalised. Then, right on half-time, an error by Willie Miller sent Völler clean through but Leighton saved superbly.

Four minutes into the second half Klaus Allofs gave West Germany the lead, so, forced to chase the game, Ferguson threw on McAvennie and Davie Cooper. Only a series of superb saves by Leighton kept Scotland in the game, and they should have been awarded a late penalty when Karlheinz Förster grabbed Archibald in the box following a scramble. In the last few minutes Cooper skipped past Lothar Matthäus and his superb cross was headed just over by Gough. A 2-1 defeat was unlucky and it was to be the only time that a team had lost in 90 minutes at the Mexico World Cup after taking the lead.

Incredibly, Scotland were still in the competition. Denmark thrashed Uruguay's 6-1 in Nezahualcóyotl, a result that meant a victory against the physical South Americans would send Scotland into the second round for the first time.

It was then that Ferguson later admitted he'd made a huge mistake. Against the advice of his assistant Walter Smith, he dropped captain Graeme Souness, who refused to sit on the bench. In came Paul McStay but not Jim Bett. McAvennie did not start despite him being the best finisher in the squad. Graeme Sharp came in to partner Sturrock up front and on Friday, 13 June 1986 Scotland lined up as follows:

Leighton
Gough–Miller (c)–Narey–Albiston
Strachan–Aitken–McStay–Nicol (Cooper 70)
Sharp–Sturrock (Nicholas 70)

The game got off to an explosive start as in the first minute José Batista scythed down Gordon Strachan. French referee Joël Quiniou produced the fastest red card in World Cup history and Scotland would now play the full match against ten men.

It was a day that cried out for the experience of Souness, who could have controlled the tempo and stood up to the roughhouse tactics of the South Americans. Instead, Uruguay kicked everything that moved. Enzo Francescoli occupied the whole Scottish back four and the constant fouling meant that the Scots could not find their rhythm. The best chance of the first half fell to Steve Nicol, who fired tamely as the goal gaped in front of him, as keeper Fernando Álvez clawed the ball from the line.

At the start of the second half Scotland forced a series of corners and free kicks that came to nothing. They seemed reluctant to throw crosses into the box, despite the prowess of Sharp. In fact, it was Uruguay who almost took the lead and only a brilliant save by Leighton kept out Wilmar Cabrera's powerful header from a free kick.

On 70 minutes Ferguson sent on Davie Cooper and Charlie Nicholas as a last throw of the dice. The Uruguayans doubled up on the winger and Nicholas received no service. Incredibly, Scotland did not have a shot on target in the whole of the second half; the closest they came to the all-important goal was a late long-range effort from David Narey that flew over. At full time Scotland were out after a 0-0 draw.

FIFA fined the South Americans and warned about their future conduct. Diego Maradona's Argentina beat them 1-0 in the last 16, before going on to beat England 2-1 thanks to the infamous 'Hand of God' goal, and the 'Goal of the Century' run and dribble by Maradona. Argentina beat Belgium 2-0 in the semi-finals and overcame West Germany 3-2 in the final. Alex Ferguson resigned straight after the game and SFA secretary Ernie Walker claimed, 'We have gone out to the scum of world football.'

In truth, it was another huge opportunity lost. The Scots only scored one goal in three games and their lack of firepower still continues to this day, as witnessed by the national team's recent Euro 2024 campaign, where a lack of goals came back to haunt them once again.

1

Andy Who?

SPECULATION SOON turned to who would take over from Alex Ferguson. The favourites were Billy McNeill and Jim McLean, with Jock Wallace also mentioned, while the media speculated on a big-name manager. Instead, the SFA chose Andy Roxburgh, who had led Scotland to victory at the 1982 UEFA European Under-18 Championship. Roxburgh had never played football at the highest level. He was a former teacher and, although highly regarded at UEFA as a technical director, he was little known to both players and the press.

In *Match* magazine on 2 August 1986, under the headline 'I'm no novice', Roxburgh stated, 'I may not have been a well-known player or club manager, but I've certainly been over the course. The SFA have groomed me for this during the past ten years and I'll be putting my body and soul into the job. I'm ready.'

He insisted on calling himself a coach and soon set about trying to qualify Scotland for Euro 88 in West Germany. They faced a very tough task in a powerful group featuring Belgium, the Republic of Ireland, Bulgaria and Luxembourg.

Andy Roxburgh was born 5 August 1943 in Glasgow. As a teenager he played for Glasgow Schools as a striker and in 1961 scored the only goal against England Schools at Celtic Park. He played for Queen's Park and later East Stirlingshire, then Patrick Thistle, staying at Firhill until 1969. Roxburgh qualified as a Scottish Football Association coach in 1966 aged just 25.

The move to Falkirk then followed, where he teamed up with another striker, Alex Ferguson. They were crowned Second Division champions in 1969/70; Roxburgh left in 1977 and then finished his career at Clydebank, where he was a player-coach and also worked as a physical education and primary school teacher from 1973 to 1975.

As the SFA's first director of coaching he was responsible for the Scotland youth teams from under-21 level down. In 1978 he led Scotland to the semi-finals of the European Under-18 Championship. Progress continued and four years later Roxburgh's team won Scotland's only tournament at UEFA level. In a 2020 BBC documentary, *The Lost Final*, Pat Nevin – a scorer in the victory over Czechoslovakia in the final – brought the squad together again, and managed to find rare archive footage of the game. Players, like captain Paul McStay, would go on to have long careers with the senior team for many years.

'Scotland at that stage were always quite competitive in the under-age national teams,' said Roxburgh, speaking to the BBC Sport website in 2022. 'I don't think we went there thinking we're going to win the trophy. This was to expose the players to international competition.'

Roxburgh may not have had expectations of lifting the trophy, but despite being without Aberdeen's Neale Cooper and Eric Black, who were absent because of club commitments, the likes of Gary Mackay, Dave Bowman, Paul McStay and Pat Nevin ensured the squad was not short on quality.

'It got massive publicity back in Scotland,' Nevin told BBC Sport. The winger, named player of the tournament, continued, 'We knew nothing about the buzz back home. I probably should have told my girlfriend I was going. I told her I was away studying and there I am on the back page of the papers. We had a lot of right good players. It was damned obvious that Paul McStay was going to make it and do well.'

Nevin was one of the few players in Roxburgh's squad not signed as a professional, and he wasn't sure he'd get a game in Finland. 'I was a part-time footballer at Clyde and a full-time business studies student, that was my mindset,' said Nevin. There were probably team talks where I wasn't concentrating because I was thinking about economic theory.'

Others were more focused on football. Centre-back Neale Cooper and forward Eric Black had both established themselves as part of Alex Ferguson's Aberdeen side, so much so that they, along with goalkeeper Bryan Gunn, were unavailable for the finals because of a clash with the Scottish Cup Final against Rangers.

All three had been part of the team that beat England 3-2 on aggregate to qualify thanks to a 1-0 win at Ibrox followed by a 2-2 draw in Coventry. 'That was the moment people started to think "oh aye, this lot are no bad",' recalled Roxburgh. 'But the Aberdeen boys being out put a dampener on things because they were the spine of the team.'

Their absence called for a little ingenuity on the part of the coach and his assistant, Walter Smith. 'We had no-clear-cut striker, so we ended up being ahead of our time by playing what they'd now call a "false nine",' Roxburgh told BBC Sport.

Nevin and Tottenham prodigy Ally Dick were the two furthest forward players, but they were detailed to occupy wide areas, with Hearts midfielder Gary Mackay breaking into the space between them.

And the plan worked. Albania were thrashed 3-0 in the opening group game, then Turkey were eased aside 2-0, meaning a draw with the Netherlands would be enough to advance. 'I sent Walter to watch them,' Roxburgh said. 'He came back and said, "No chance. The boy Marco van Basten is magnificent, Gerald Vanenburg in midfield is terrific and the goalkeeper is outstanding." And I remember saying we'd just have to fight them, in that case.'

Van Basten gave the Dutch the lead, but a late leveller by Dundee United defender Gary McGinnis put the Scots through. Ally Dick, who went on to sign for Ajax, remembers future team-mate Van Basten grumbling about the outcome years later. The point secured a semi-final with Poland, beaten finalists 12 months earlier. 'You could tell five or ten minutes in "we can do them",' Nevin said of the Poles. And the Scots did, earning a comfortable 2-0 victory to set up a final with Czechoslovakia.

But Nevin had a problem: he was scheduled to have a university exam the afternoon after the final: 'When we reached the semis, I was gutted because I had to knuckle down to my studying. I worked out I could manage both if we reached the final, but my one worry was that the plane would be delayed.'

Goals from Mackay, Nevin and John Philliben secured a straightforward 3-1 victory and ensured that Scotland would be crowned European champions. 'It was brilliant,' said Brian Rice, a member of the squad. 'We were only babies, so we weren't able to drink officially. We found a bar in the small town we were in, had something to eat, then some of us had a couple of drinks and had a carry-on and a singsong.'

Hibernian midfielder Rice, who had played in two of the group games, was restored for the final because Jim McInally of Celtic was suspended, and was deployed in an unfamiliar left-back role. 'I was a wee bit tentative; it's OK for your youth team but this was a European final,' said Rice, who went on to play in England with Nottingham Forest and later became head coach at Hamilton Academical. 'I didn't want to be the one who made a mistake and cost the team a goal, but everything turned out all right.'

'It was a really difficult game,' said Nevin. 'I can't remember the other goals but I remember mine. We had a free kick outside the box and the idea was someone was to pass to someone else who was to lay it off for someone else to shoot. The lads got utterly confused by it.

'The ball landed at my feet with four defenders just sprinting straight at me. I dribbled through and put the ball away to score. Anybody watching would have thought it was a technically organised piece of football but it was nothing of the sort.'

Nevin dodged the celebrations and 'went straight to my room and my books' before catching his flight the next morning and ambling straight from the airport to the university exam hall, where he was met by his gawping peers. This, after all, was a young man who had scored a stunning goal for Scotland in a major final the night before.

Scotland's team for the final was Robin Rae (Hibernian), Dave Beaumont (Dundee United), John Philliben (Stirling

Albion), David Rennie (Leicester City), Brian Rice (Hibernian), Paul McStay (Celtic), Dave Bowman (Hearts), Gary McGinnis (Dundee United), Pat Nevin (Clyde), Gary Mackay (Hearts), Ally Dick (Tottenham). The substitutes were Ian Westwater (Hearts), Billy Livingstone (Wolves) and Sammy McGivern (Kilmarnock). Jim Dobbin missed the game through injury and Celtic team-mate Jim McInally was suspended.

As European champions, the Scots would go to Mexico for the 1983 FIFA World Youth Championship with their eyes on the title – and with good reason. An already talented group were burnished by the return of Aberdeen trio Cooper, Black and Gunn, who were absent in Finland, as well as the addition of St Mirren's Steve Clarke, Dave McPherson of Rangers and Motherwell's Brian McClair.

The Scots started their group with a laboured win over South Korea, before travelling north to Toluca for their second match, against Australia. The temperature was recorded as 30°C in a city sitting more than 2,500 metres above sea level and the Scots toiled. Despite a goal from Paul McStay, Roxburgh's side would fall to a listless 2-1 defeat.

In a 2022 article in *The Guardian*, Brian Rice recalled, 'The ball was flying all over the place because the air was so thin and I'd never experienced humidity like it. I was a sub and I remember boys getting oxygen masks at half-time because they were done.'

Qualification came down to a daunting final group game against hosts Mexico, one that those who were there will never forget. Steve Clarke, a youngster then and eventually the head coach of the full Scotland national team, called the occasion 'the night I realised I could be a professional player'. Rice said it was 'bedlam, mayhem, mental', and

Roxburgh recalled that 'boys literally became men' in the seething bowl of the Azteca Stadium. Official records state that 86,582 people – almost exclusively ferocious Mexicans – were inside the ground but it seemed like much, much more to the callow Scots.

'Just driving up to the stadium, there were people everywhere making a racket,' said Rice. 'Then to even be on the pitch during the warm-up, here were these wee guys from Scotland playing in the ground where Brazil had won the World Cup 13 years earlier. I remember making a point of putting the ball in the net where Pelé scored and it was surreal.' That would be Rice's only involvement on the pitch, but even those on the bench had to keep their wits about them as a bombardment of projectiles were hurled from the stands in a barrage that intensified when Clarke scored the only goal to edge Scotland into the quarter-finals.

'I took the corner, and it was dreadful,' said Nevin to *The Scotsman* in 2022. 'But that game has stuck with me, despite playing another 850-odd times in my career. I learned that night if you're not spooked when a crowd of that size are physically trying to attack you, then nothing will ever bother you.'

The Scots couldn't get out of the stadium for some time after the match but they cared not a jot, given that the result had won the group and set up a reunion with Poland. But, by then, Roxburgh's group of teenagers were physically and emotionally spent and could not summon the resolve to recover from an early concession against the Poles in a last-eight tie that ended in a 1-0 defeat. Poland would go on to lose to Argentina, who in turn lost the final to a Brazil team containing future stars such as Bebeto, Jorginho and Dunga.

Walter Smith believed Roxburgh did not get the credit he deserved for his work with that squad and that the achievement had been forgotten. The manager was also the Scottish FA director of coaching at the time and showed his assistant a report he had produced warning that changes in society would cause the number of players to dwindle.

In *The Guardian*, Roxburgh, technical director of the Asian Football Confederation at the time of writing, reflected with great fondness on that astonishing 12 months for his squad, 'You don't spend on youth football; you invest and hope you get a good return. And with that group we did, and then some. It's a big part of the reason I got the national team job and it's the best job I ever had, going on this adventure with these young players.'

2

Scotland 1986/87

ON 10 SEPTEMBER 1986, Scotland welcomed Bulgaria
to Hampden for their first Euro 88 qualifier. A good start
was vital and Andy Roxburgh picked a bold attacking side
including wingers Gordon Strachan and Davie Cooper with
an exciting-looking partnership of Charlie Nicholas and Mo
Johnston up front. In front of a crowd of 35,000, Scotland
found it hard to break down the resolute Bulgarian defence.
In a first half of few chances, a fine save denied Cooper,
and Bulgaria went close after a fine flowing move. After the
interval Cooper went on a brilliant mazy run and put the
ball on a plate for Paul McStay, who fired narrowly wide.
Roxburgh threw on Kenny Dalglish in the 53rd minute for
Nicholas but to no avail. Jim Leighton saved well late on and
the game ended goalless. It was a frustrating start.

Next up in October was a tough away game against Jack
Charlton's Republic of Ireland in Dublin. Lansdowne Road,
the home of the Irish rugby union team, had no floodlights,
so international games were played in the afternoon. On
a notoriously poor pitch, to combat their direct style of
play Roxburgh drafted in David Narey and Alan Hansen
to play alongside Richard Gough in a three-man defence.

Graeme Sharp partnered Johnston up front. In a game of few chances, Ireland went closest when Alan Hansen headed off the line from Kevin Sheedy. In the second half Leighton saved well from a Paul McGrath header, as Liam Brady began to run the midfield. In the closing minutes Frank Stapleton fired over, but Scotland, who created little, got the point they wanted after a 0-0 draw.

As Scotland went into their next game at home to Luxembourg their goal drought was the main topic of conversation: they had now scored only once in their last six internationals. So back came Dalglish for his 102nd and final cap; Johnston and Brian McClair also started, with Pat Nevin and Davie Cooper providing the width. Scotland started confidently; Nevin was a constant threat and it was his fine run that led to a penalty, confidently dispatched by Cooper in the 24th minute. Dalglish was denied a national record 31st goal after a flying header was brilliantly saved, but Cooper settled any nerves when he scored again after 38 minutes. In the second half McClair went close and Ally McCoist came on as a third striker. On 70 minutes Mo Johnston headed home a corner as Scotland ran out 3-0 winners. Roxburgh was satisfied by the victory but knew that tougher tests were to come.

On 18 February 1987 Scotland faced the Republic of Ireland at Hampden. There was a huge away support, largely made up of Celtic fans. Roxburgh knew that this game was pivotal and picked a very attacking line-up. Hansen partnered Gough in central defence, on his 26th and final appearance for his country. Gordon Strachan, Cooper and Nevin supported Johnston and McClair up front. Jack Charlton picked a powerful team full of defenders. Scotland dominated possession but created little, with Mick

McCarthy and Paul McGrath dominant while Strachan, in particular, kept giving the ball away. The only goal came in the eighth minute when Mark Lawrenson converted a quickly taken free kick.

Roxburgh sent on McStay and McCoist but they could not get into the game. Late on, Johnston burst through but his shot was cleared off the line and the Republic of Ireland claimed a famous 1-0 victory. It was a devastating blow that effectively killed off Scotland's qualifying hopes.

In April, Scotland went to Brussels to face World Cup semi-finalists Belgium. They needed at least a point to keep their faint Euro 88 dreams alive. With Bulgaria and Ireland both well placed, the odds were against Roxburgh's men. Scotland lined up in their lemon-yellow away kit for the last time. Their team had an unfamiliar look: David Narey partnered Alex McLeish in central defence and Jim Bett returned in midfield. On eight minutes Nico Claesen beat the Scottish offside trap to fire Belgium ahead. Their lead did not last long, however, as Bett crossed and Paul McStay headed the equaliser five minutes later. The Scottish midfield looked far too open and were unable to stop Enzo Scifo from pulling the strings. Early in the second half Tottenham striker Claesen scored following a corner. Worse was to come as Franky Vercauteren swept home a third. Nevin replaced Jim Bett with ten minutes to go but Claesen completed his hat-trick on 85 minutes, after he outpaced McLeish. A 4-1 defeat was Scotland's worst since losing by the same score to Brazil in the 1982 World Cup.

Roxburgh pointed out that the Scots had played well in the first half and were caught by goals on the break. However, he was now under pressure. He had won just once in his first five games in charge and critics questioned whether the job was too much for him. Captain Roy Aitken came to his defence and pointed out that the players were to blame for the poor results and they were right behind their manager.

Things were not going to get any easier and next up was the Rous Cup. Brazil had been invited to play alongside England and few expected the Scots to get anything from their more illustrious opponents.

On 23 May England came to Hampden on a hot Saturday afternoon. They had drawn 1-1 with Brazil at Wembley and were favourites to sweep the Scots aside. Gary Lineker, who had headed home against Brazil, was unavailable as he had a league game for Barcelona that evening. Alongside Peter Beardsley, who was to make a £1.9m British record transfer to Liverpool a few weeks later, was Mark Hateley, about to join Monaco alongside Glenn Hoddle under their young coach Arsène Wenger.

Scotland lined up with Willie Miller and Alex McLeish back together in central defence and it made a huge difference. Aitken was joined by Paul McStay, Neil Simpson and Leicester winger Ian Wilson, who was making his debut. In attack, Brian McClair, soon to join Manchester United, was partnered by Rangers striker Ally McCoist.

Leighton
Gough–Miller–McLeish–MacLeod
McStay–Simpson–Aitken (c)–Wilson
McClair (Nicholas 58)–McCoist

England had Rangers keeper Chris Woods and his club captain Terry Butcher at the back, alongside Mark Wright. Despite just winning the championship with Rangers, Butcher was roundly booed. In midfield, captain Bryan

Robson had Hoddle alongside him with Chris Waddle providing the width. A crowd of 64,000 packed into Hampden and the game was live on the BBC's *Grandstand*.

The first half was a scrappy affair; Jim Leighton parried a shot by Hateley and Robson headed wide. Richard Gough fired a weak shot straight at Woods and MacLeod also failed to test the England goalkeeper from long range.

At the start of the second half the game began to open up more. Robson fired into the side netting from the edge of the box after a fine run by Waddle, then Scotland almost took the lead when Butcher charged down a shot by McCoist and Woods gathered after a scramble in the area. Beardsley was denied by Jim Leighton after he burst through and Andy Roxburgh threw on Charlie Nicholas for McClair on the hour. It was a match crying out for the skill of Davie Cooper to run at a tired-looking England defence, but he stayed on the bench. Arsenal striker Nicholas went closest to breaking the deadlock in the last 15 minutes, striking the crossbar from close range with Woods beaten. Leighton saved well from Waddle's header and Scotland held on for a goalless draw. It was a creditable performance and the first 0-0 draw between the two sides since 1970.

It meant that the Scotland v Brazil fixture would decide the destiny of the Rous Cup. A disappointing crowd of 41,000 turned up hoping to see Scotland's first victory over the three-times World Cup winners. Their team lacked the flair of previous years but they were still a formidable proposition. They had suffered a 1-0 defeat in Dublin a few weeks before, Liam Brady scoring the Republic of Ireland's winner in a friendly.

Roxburgh rang the changes: Andy Goram replaced Jim Leighton in goal with Cooper back on the left wing. Scotland played well in the first half; Aitken and McStay linked well in midfield, while Cooper troubled the Brazilian defence with his runs. McCoist went close but on 51 minutes Brazil took the lead. Raí, the younger brother of Sócrates, scored the opener, after Goram failed to hold a curling shot. On the hour Valdo put the game beyond the Scots, after he broke clear and fired past Goram. Although Scotland huffed and puffed, they never looked like getting back into the game and Brazil held on for a comfortable 2-0 victory. They lifted the Rous Cup wearing their swapped Scotland shirts.

It had been a difficult season for Andy Roxburgh, whose team had won just once in seven games. They suffered defeats against the Republic of Ireland and Belgium that destroyed their hopes of qualifying for Euro 88. Goalscoring was still a problem, the team hitting the back of the net just four times.

At the back, I think it seemed clear that the partnership of Willie Miller and Alex McLeish was the best available and Roy Aitken proved to be an able captain. Paul McStay had formed a promising partnership with him, but up front Roxburgh still had to find the right blend. Brian McClair and Ally McCoist had yet to score for their country. Mo Johnston was still the best striker available but Charlie Nicholas and the veteran Kenny Dalglish did not seem to be the answer.

On 9 September 1987 Hungary visited Hampden for a friendly. In his programme notes, Roxburgh stated, 'The next World Cup starts here,' as he outlined his plans to put a squad together to qualify for the 1990 finals in Italy.

He was prepared to experiment and bring new players into the team and a crowd of 35,000 saw a new-look line-up. Steve Clarke made his debut at right-back; at the time he was making a name for himself at Chelsea, after moving down from St Mirren. Ian Durrant also made his debut, the exciting 20-year-old Rangers midfielder lining up alongside Old Firm rivals Aitken and McStay. Up front were Johnston and McCoist. The Rangers striker had yet to find the net in six previous games for his country.

After a promising opening McStay went close with a shot well saved, then Durrant nearly opened the scoring, but a fine save denied him after he linked up well with Johnston. The visitors continued to threaten on the break and Leighton saved well from Gyula Hajszán. Peter then brought out a superb flying save by Leighton. In the 34th minute McCoist fired Scotland ahead from a free kick, his first goal in dark blue. Péter Disztl was at full stretch to deny Strachan, and Johnston miskicked from point-blank range.

In the second half the Scots continued to press, and in the 61st minute Durrant sent McCoist through to round Disztl before firing confidently into the net. The Hungarians refused to lie down and captain Imre Garaba forced Leighton to tip a long-range effort around the post. Eric Black replaced Johnston, and Jim Bett came on for McStay in the last 20 minutes. Durrant fired wide when well placed but the Scots were good value for a 2-0 victory. Andy Roxburgh hailed an encouraging performance, a solid debut by Clarke, some good touches by Durrant and a lively front line of McCoist and Johnston.

In October Belgium came to Hampden. They still had an outside chance of qualifying for Euro 88 and Roxburgh gave a debut to Gary Gillespie of Liverpool alongside Alex McLeish at centre-back. Clarke and Durrant kept their places and Ian Wilson, now of Everton, came in on the left wing. Scotland had not beaten Belgium at home since 1971, Kenny Dalglish's debut.

A crowd of just 20,000 were present and they saw the Scots take the lead after 14 minutes. Wilson flicked on Clarke's cross and Johnston headed back to McCoist who beat Michel Preud'homme, as the Belgian defence appealed in vain for offside. McStay fired over after a well-worked free kick before the visitors pushed forward in search of an equaliser. He was linking up well with Durrant and in the second half Wilson began to find some joy down the left. A diving header by McCoist was well saved and then Derek Whyte replaced Maurice Malpas to earn his first cap. Graeme Sharp came on for Johnston, who came in for some rough treatment by the Belgian defence. In the 79th minute, McStay, who had had an outstanding match, ran through on the edge of the box to side-foot home. Clarke then sent McCoist through but he was denied by a fine save. A 2-0 victory capped the best performance so far under Andy Roxburgh's reign; a promising debut by Gillespie, Durrant neat and tidy on the ball and the strike force of Johnston and McCoist again looking sharp and dangerous.

3

The Real Mackay

IN NOVEMBER, Scotland flew to Sofia to face Bulgaria in their penultimate Group 7 game. They had nothing to play for but the fixture would be decisive, as a win or draw would send the Eastern Europeans through to Euro 88 in West Germany, while a Scotland victory would send Jack Charlton's Republic of Ireland to the Euros for the first time in their history. It would turn out to be the first time that the Irish had qualified for a major tournament.

The task ahead looked tough for Charlton. To qualify, Ireland would have to win a group that contained Belgium, Bulgaria and Scotland, three sides that had played in the 1986 World Cup. Ireland started slowly in the group; Liam Brady scored a last-minute penalty to secure a 2-2 draw in Belgium; then after a goalless draw with Scotland in Dublin, they secured their first win at Hampden Park. Another draw with Belgium and two wins over Luxembourg continued the improvement, but defeat in Bulgaria to another late penalty appeared to have put a big dent in their hopes of reaching the finals.

As Ireland prepared for their last group match, at home to Bulgaria in October 1987, qualification was still possible, but only if three things happened: Ireland needed to beat Bulgaria, Scotland had to take at least a point off Belgium on the same day, and then Scotland had to win in Bulgaria. Not much to ask for. Ireland kept their part of the bargain by beating Bulgaria 2-0. When Scotland defeated Belgium by the same scoreline later that evening, their hopes grew. But there was one final hurdle in front of Charlton and the signs were not promising: Bulgaria had not lost a qualifier in Sofia since 1982. Scotland's away record was poor and injuries were decimating Andy Roxburgh's plans. 'At their best, the Scots are capable of beating anybody but Bulgaria are a strong, competitive team who don't normally lose at home,' midfielder Brady told the *Irish Times*.

Rangers trio Richard Gough, Ian Durrant and Ally McCoist pulled out of Scotland's squad to face Ireland on 11 November because of injuries, while Mo Johnston was also unavailable due to club commitments with Nantes. Many Irish fans settled down to watch the match on RTE more in hope than expectation.

Few expected anything from the Scots; for Roxburgh it was an opportunity to build on the Belgium victory and blood some new players. On a wet and grey evening at the Vasil Levski National Stadium, 49,976 fans packed into the ground in anticipation. Only a few hundred of the Tartan Army made the trip. Bulgaria had reached the last 16 of the 1986 World Cup, drawing with Italy and South Korea before losing to hosts Mexico. They were an experienced team, solid in defence with a young Hristo Stoichkov leading their attack alongside Nasko Sirakov.

Scotland lined up with:

Leighton
Clarke–Gillespie–McLeish–Malpas
Nicol–McStay (Mackay 57)–Aitken (c)–Wilson
Sharp (Durie 71)–McClair

Bulgaria had not lost at home for three years. The Scots started with just two Old Firm players – captain Roy Aitken and Paul McStay, both of Celtic. After Durrant, Gough and McCoist withdrew through injury, there were no Rangers players in the starting 11.

Scotland had not won an away match since January 1986 when they beat Israel 1-0 in a friendly. Packed with defenders, it was clear that they were going there to be dogged and stubborn opponents. Graeme Sharp and Brian McClair had yet to score for their country. Two excellent strikers for Everton and Manchester United, it remains a mystery why they could not find their scoring boots at international level.

The Bulgarians began at a frantic pace. In just the second minute, Jim Leighton made a superb save, as the Scots struggled to get a foothold in the game. On a rain-soaked, muddy pitch, the home side knocked the ball around confidently. Sharp and McClair were isolated up front, though they battled well. Aitken made a powerful run through the centre but was flagged offside. The referee regularly stopped the game after a series of niggly fouls, so it was hard for either team to build any momentum. Sharp broke well on the left and his dangerous cross was dealt with by the Bulgaria defence. Steve Nicol, playing on the right side of midfield, was linking up well with Steve Clarke as the Scots tried to threaten on the break.

In the 25th minute Stoichkov fired just wide from a free kick on the edge of the box. As the game wore on

Aitken began to dominate in midfield, and on 30 minutes Ian Wilson's corner was dropped by Borislav Mihaylov and he then gathered a tame shot by Aitken. Sirakov went close when he controlled the ball well but fired just over. Alex McLeish was dominant in the air with Gary Gillespie looking assured alongside him. With the hosts content to keep possession, the first half ended scoreless.

At half-time Gary Mackay of Hearts replaced the injured Paul McStay for his debut. McClair drifted into midfield leaving Sharp as the lone Scottish striker. The large home crowd were subdued the longer the game went on, and the nerves crept into the players with their goal in sight. Strangely, a large section of the stand was full of Bulgarian soldiers in their green uniforms. With about 20 minutes left, Bulgaria began to run down the clock, playing the ball along their back four and committing a series of petty fouls.

Chelsea's Gordon Durie replaced Sharp to make his debut. Scotland almost took the lead when McClair burst through on the right, but he took too long to find Durie and the chance was gone. Then in the 87th minute Stoichkov hacked down Durie on the touchline, but Austrian referee Helmut Kohl played the advantage, and Mackay collected Clarke's pass, burst through and fired into the far corner.

In an article in *The Guardian* from November 2014, he recalled, 'All I was concerned about was trying to make an impact as an individual.' In the same article, Bulgarian goalkeeper Mihaylov lamented, 'When I saw the ball behind me, my heart stopped.'

As Bulgaria threw men forward desperately in search of an equaliser, McClair fired straight at Mihaylov. In injury time Sirakov shot just wide and, despite four minutes added on, Scotland held on for a famous 1-0 victory which ultimately sent the Republic of Ireland through to the Euro 88 finals. Bulgarian manager Hristo Mladenov was soon sacked and Mihaylov described it as the worst moment of his career.

Post-match, Andy Roxburgh told the *Daily Record*, 'In congratulating the Irish, I don't wish to sound mean when I say we lost to them in highly controversial circumstances at Hampden Park last February. We threw away our chances of qualifying by surrendering points we ought to have won. But while I would like to have taken the team to the European finals, there is at least a consolation that we finished our programme in style.'

'Scotland's victory over Bulgaria in Sofia yesterday won no prizes for beauty but to Irish eyes it was sweet indeed,' reported *The Guardian*. 'Charlton had proven the doubters wrong and, like he predicted, he would be judged on results.'

Jack Charlton himself admitted, 'Lest anybody forget this job is only half done. Qualifying is one thing but we must go to the finals determined to justify our presence in them.' They would do that and more the following summer, famously beating England 1-0 with Glasgow-born Ray Houghton's header. A creditable 1-1 draw with eventual runners-up the Soviet Union and a narrow 1-0 defeat to eventual winners the Netherlands meant Charlton's men did Ireland proud, and they returned to a hero's welcome in Dublin.

The Irish FA sent a crate of champagne to the Scottish FA, who returned it. Gary Mackay would win a total of four caps, in a long career in which he played a record 737 times for Hearts. Sitting in an Edinburgh studio he was later presented with a special award by broadcaster RTE at their Sports Person of the Year awards.

Scotland completed their Group 7 campaign with a visit to Luxembourg on 2 December. Typically, as is so often the case in their history, they failed to perform against the so-called minnows and could only manage a frustrating 0-0 draw.

Group 7 final table:

	P	W	D	L	F	A	Pts
Republic of Ireland	8	4	3	1	10	5	11
Bulgaria	8	4	2	2	12	6	10
Belgium	8	3	3	2	16	8	9
Scotland	8	3	3	2	7	5	9
Luxembourg	8	0	1	7	2	23	1

For Andy Roxburgh there were some signs of encouragement; Scotland had kept five clean sheets in eight games; however they were still goal shy, netting just seven times.

As would befit a former teacher, Roxburgh was a very studious and organised coach. He paid huge attention to detail. Charlie Nicholas said in a radio interview in 1987, 'Andy had organised a meeting about a meeting!' Former players described him as very serious without a great sense of humour.

His new assistant, Craig Brown, was a genial character and himself a former teacher. Born in Glasgow in 1940, Brown had a modest career at Dundee and Falkirk. After a knee injury ended his time as a player early, he decided to go into coaching. He became assistant manager of Motherwell in 1974. He got his first managerial job as part-time manager of Clyde in 1977 where he spent ten seasons, winning the Second Division championship in his first season – alongside working as a primary school headteacher, then a lecturer in primary education at Craigie College, Ayr.

In 1986, after being part of the coaching staff at the World Cup, Brown took charge of Scotland's youth teams. In 1989, he coached the under-16s to the final of the 1989 FIFA U-16 World Championship. Three years later he coached the under-21s to the semi-finals of the 1992 UEFA U-21 European Championship. In July 1986, he took up the post of assistant manager of Scotland, also with responsibility for the under-21 team. Brown served alongside Andy Roxburgh at the 1990 World Cup and at Euro 92.

Not all of the players responded well to Roxburgh's approach. Steve Nicol complained that he treated the players as children, constantly telling them to tuck their shirts in and straighten their socks. As a UEFA technical director Roxburgh had a vast knowledge of European football. He prepared diligently for every game, watching opponents in person or on video and preparing dossiers on tactics for each opponent. That gave the players confidence whenever they went out on to the pitch.

4

Wembley Woe

ON 17 FEBRUARY 1988 Scotland travelled to Saudi Arabia to play a lucrative friendly. Eyebrows were raised at the timing of the match, right into the main part of the season and inevitably Andy Roxburgh faced several call-offs. He was still able to select a strong starting 11, notable for the return of Celtic striker Frank McAvennie for the first time in three years, for his fifth and final cap. The game would also see the debut of the skilful Hibernian midfielder John Collins.

The hosts began with a confident display of possession football, and on 15 minutes Jim Leighton made a superb save from Yousef Jazah's rasping free kick. From the resulting corner he headed Saudi Arabia into the lead after Leighton came and missed the ball. The goal stunned the visitors, who were creating little in the stifling heat. At half-time Roxburgh rang the changes. In came Henry Smith in goal for his debut, as did Hearts winger John Colquhoun, with Alex McLeish also replacing Willie Miller.

Just two minutes into the second half Mo Johnston rose unmarked to head home the equaliser from Paul McStay's cross. The striker had joined Nantes at the start of the

1987/88 season and had lost none of his finishing ability. The 30,000 crowd, with a large contingent of British fans who worked in the oil industry, had more to cheer in the 49th minute as Collins curled home a superb free kick from the edge of the box to give the Scots a 2-1 lead. Gary Mackay replaced McStay just after the hour, as the midfield, with captain Roy Aitken in particular, seemed to fade in the afternoon sun. On 71 minutes Majed Abdullah ran on to a simple long pass and bundled the ball over the line after Smith and Maurice Malpas failed to clear. Johnston and McAvennie were isolated up front and although Collins continued to probe away, the game ended in a very disappointing 2-2 draw.

Post-match, Roxburgh pointed to the heat and the makeshift nature of the starting 11, but following on from a goalless draw in Luxembourg, it was a frustrating display and result. Despite his promising debut, Collins would not win another cap for two years. Scotland did not have time to dwell on that result as in March they travelled to Malta to play another friendly. It was another chance to experiment and bring in some younger players. Rangers midfielder Derek Ferguson, whose younger brother Barry would later go on to captain club and country, made his first start, with a new-look strike force of Graeme Sharp and Ally McCoist in attack.

For Sharp it would be a 12th and final international appearance but he signed off with a goal, a good header after 21 minutes. The main problem for Roxburgh was a lack of service and goals from midfield. Although a fine captain, Roy Aitken was never prolific; in fact, he only ever scored once for his country in 57 appearances. Paul McStay, their main creative influence, who would have a long Scotland career stretching from 1983 to 1997, found it hard to play consistently at international level. He would go on to score nine times in 76 games.

Roxburgh favoured more defensive midfielders like Steve Nicol and although he was instrumental in bringing Pat Nevin through from the youth setup, he did not often pick the skilful Chelsea winger. Davie Cooper was phased out of the team and with a lack of goals and creativity in midfield, it was no wonder that the constant chopping and changing in attack had yet to find the right combination.

Scotland failed to build on their early lead as Malta equalised on 54 minutes, and although Roxburgh threw on McClair and Colquhoun, the Scots had to settle for a 1-1 draw. The momentum and confidence that the team had gained from the excellent wins over Belgium and Bulgaria had been lost. Roxburgh was left scratching his head, and pointed to the fact that he was trying to bring through younger players, and it would take time for them to find their feet at international level. He also believed that players found it hard to motivate themselves for friendly games, especially against weaker opposition. He maintained that against better opposition and in qualifying games when it really mattered, the players would rise to the occasion.

In April, Scotland arrived in Spain for a glamorous friendly at the Santiago Bernabéu Stadium in Madrid. Sadly, a crowd of just 15,000 turned up. Roxburgh picked a team full of defenders in a 5-3-2 formation:

Leighton
Gough–Miller–McLeish–Gillespie–Nicol
McStay–Aitken (c)–Durrant
Johnston–McCoist

Spain, who had qualified for Euro 88, began the game confidently, with Michel to the fore. Emilio Butragueño, the Real Madrid striker nicknamed 'The Vulture', looked sharp as the Scots struggled to get into the game. Leighton saved well from both of them as Scotland defended a series of corners. Ian Durrant probed but Johnston and McCoist could not find any space in attack. McStay was subdued and Scotland's best chance was when Roy Aitken ran through the Spanish defence but dragged his shot wide. Early in the second half Richard Gough moved forward more and was a threat from corners. Leighton had to be at his agile best to save late on from Michel and Julio Salinas, but at full time Scotland had earned a creditable 0-0 draw. Roxburgh was pleased with his side's battling qualities, but the same could not be said of the home fans, with bottles and coins thrown when the visitors' coach left the stadium.

In May, the season ended with the annual Rous Cup, between England, Scotland and, this year, Colombia. The South Americans were an unknown quantity and a crowd of just 20,000 welcomed them to Hampden Park. Scotland unveiled their new strip of blue shirts with white collars, white shorts and red socks – traditional colours. It was good to see the back of the awful white shorts with blue hoops.

With Wembley in mind a few days later, Andy Roxburgh went for an experienced line-up. Dundee United winger Kevin Gallacher made his debut, with Mo Johnston as the established number nine. With a subdued atmosphere, Scotland found it hard to settle. Colombia, with Carlos Valderrama – famous for his extravagant hairstyle – were skilful and kept the ball well. In goal, the eccentric René Higuita was often dribbling the ball into midfield and had little to do in the first 25 minutes. Gradually, McStay began to find his passing range. Gallacher's pace caused problems but Johnston got little change from Andrés Escobar. Murdo MacLeod was a solid presence on the left, but the game got bogged down in midfield, with the flow interrupted by a series of fouls.

In the second half Derek Ferguson replaced McCoist and in-form Celtic striker Andy Walker made his debut, replacing Gallacher. The Scots huffed and puffed but failed to test Higuita. The closest they came to breaking the deadlock was a late McStay free kick that flew wide. The goalless draw was a fair result but the lack of creativity was a concern.

On 21 May 1988 Scotland faced England at Wembley. After qualifying impressively for Euro 88, scoring an impressive 19 goals and conceding just once, Bobby Robson's team were one of the favourites for European glory. It was the first time the old rivals would meet on a Saturday afternoon since 1981, when the Scots triumphed thanks to a John Robertson penalty. Their previous visits in 1983 and 1986 were typically competitive but midweek nights, designed to curb the thousands of travelling Scotland fans taking over central London, many drunk and without tickets. The fixture had lost much of its importance, with World Cup and Euro qualifying seen as more of a priority, and England regarding West Germany and Argentina as bigger rivals.

In 1983 Jock Stein had picked a team of hard-running and solid players, but despite new sensation Charlie Nicholas in attack, weeks before he joined Arsenal in a £750,000 deal from Celtic, they were still well beaten 2-0. The game took place on 1 June at the end of a long, hard season. The defeat led to questions being asked about Stein's position, after five years in charge. Scotland had failed to qualify for

Euro 84, and had finished bottom of their group with just one win in six matches.

England were expected to win comfortably and a crowd of 70,000 was nearly 20,000 down on capacity. Sadly, the game was marred by crowd trouble before, during and afterwards, with over 100 arrests and tragically the death of a fan.

Scotland lined up as follows:

Leighton
Gough–Miller–McLeish–Nicol
McStay–Simpson (Burns 74)–Aitken (c)–MacLeod
Johnston–McCoist (Gallacher 77)

Scotland began determined to get stuck into their opponents but after 12 minutes England took the lead. Peter Beardsley linked up well with John Barnes and chipped the ball past Jim Leighton. With Richard Gough marking Barnes, Gary Lineker found space to trouble the Scotland defence. His shot was parried by Leighton before he brilliantly saved the rebound from Beardsley. Aitken and McStay found it hard to curb the power of England captain Bryan Robson and Neil Webb and central midfield. Neil Simpson and Murdo MacLeod were both solid players alongside them, but provided little width or creativity. Webb headed straight at Leighton from a corner and Lineker was unfortunate not to be awarded a penalty after Gough brought him down.

England continued to attack in the second half and Leighton made a brilliant save from Kenny Sansom's chip. As the game wore on Scotland began to throw more men forward. Ally McCoist, feeding on scraps, shot into the side netting but neither him nor Mo Johnston made any impact on a dominant Tony Adams. Tommy Burns replaced

Neil Simpson with 16 minutes to go, before Barnes headed against the bar after Leighton punched clear Waddle's cross.

Roared on by a large Tartan Army contingent, although they enjoyed more possession Scotland barely troubled the England defence. They almost snatched an equaliser in the last few minutes when Kevin Gallacher, on for McCoist, saw his shot saved by Peter Shilton's feet, but England did enough to win 1-0. It was only a magnificent performance by Jim Leighton – who would join Alex Ferguson at Manchester United later that summer – that had kept Scotland in the game. However, Roxburgh could have few complaints about the defeat. It felt as if he and Craig Brown had gone for damage limitation with their starting line-up, but, given England's dominance, maybe they were right to be cautious.

So 1987/88 had been a mixed season for Scotland. They had only lost once in nine games, with notable victories over Belgium and Bulgaria and a creditable draw in Spain. However, poor draws against Luxembourg, Saudi Arabia and Malta followed. Defensively the Scots were impressive in keeping six clean sheets. But once again they had found it hard to score goals, netting just eight times all season and failing to score in four games.

The jury was still out on Andy Roxburgh after only four wins in his first 16 games. However, Scotland had only lost four times as well, with too many draws. But he had gained valuable experience. He had blooded some exciting young players and had tried different systems. Everything was geared to the forthcoming 1990 World Cup qualifying campaign.

5

Norwegian Opener

14 September – Norway 1 Scotland 2

SCOTLAND WERE drawn against Euro 84 winners France, Yugoslavia, Norway and Cyprus in Group 5 with the top two teams qualifying for the 1990 World Cup in Italy.

For Tartan Army regulars Paul and Jim Hamilton, a trip to Oslo was a chance to see Scotland in a place they had never visited before. Jim explained, 'We had been following Scotland abroad since 1986, although we only managed to see one game at the World Cup, the 1-0 defeat by Denmark. We had been going to Hampden since 1984 and seen some great games. To be honest, we were not sure about Andy Roxburgh and the team. Qualification wouldn't be easy so we knew a good start was vital.'

Paul remembered, 'We took the train from Edinburgh to Glasgow, then flew to Oslo the day before the game. We stayed at a youth hostel which was cheap but basic. I remember it was quite expensive [to go out in Oslo] so we didn't have too many beers. We saw some Scotland supporters in town but only a few hundred and the locals were friendly.

'The stadium was small, probably only held 25,000, and we had a section in the corner behind the goal. It was a tense game but a relief in the end.'

Andy Roxburgh decided to shuffle his pack and, to counter the aerial threat of Jan Åge Fjørtoft, in came Gary Gillespie of Liverpool. Steve Nicol was on the left side of midfield. Kevin Gallacher also got a start, to provide pace and width on the right. Brian McClair partnered Mo Johnston up front, the pair working together as they had done at Celtic. Although he would have taken a point before the game, Roxburgh knew a win was vital, as he expected France and Yugoslavia to take maximum points from the Norwegians.

Leighton
Gillespie–Miller–McLeish–Malpas
Gallacher–Aitken (c) (Durrant 68)–McStay–Nicol
Johnston–McClair

Scotland kicked off and the game was a few minutes old when Norway's midfield general, Greece-based Tom Sundby, was tackled by Steve Nicol. It looked innocuous but Sundby stayed down, clearly in a lot of pain. Clutching his right knee, he was replaced by Ørjan Berg. Powerful and direct, the hosts began strongly forcing a series of corners. Their main weapons at set pieces were the gigantic Rune Bratseth, the West Germany-based central defender, who came forward to try and win headers, and also the energetic Karl Petter Løken along their right-hand side.

The Scots had not had much to shout about early on, but there had been signs that they were growing into the contest ahead of them taking an unexpected 14th-minute lead courtesy of midfield man Paul McStay's sixth international goal. Willie Miller in the centre circle aimed a high ball into the area, Mo Johnston challenged, and it broke free towards the edge of the area, where McStay arrived and hit a first-time drive low with his left foot past Erik Thorstvedt.

The 1-0 lead meant Scotland sat back and waited to catch the hosts on the break. At times they went direct, looking for the pace of Gallacher, and McClair occasionally dropped back into midfield. He played very intelligently. He knew when to hold on to the ball, when to make a run and when to play a pass. The half was approaching its final moments when the hosts struck back. Norway won a free kick some 30 yards out and Kjetil Osvold lifted the ball into the box. It was headed away by Aitken, but it fell to Fjørtoft, who headed home the equaliser. Scotland claimed that Erland Johnsen was offside and impeding Leighton on the goal line as the ball went in. Referee Luigi Agnolin waved away their protests and it was 1-1 at half-time.

At the start of the second half the visitors had changed their shape to a midfield diamond. Gallacher moved from the right into a more central, forward position alongside Johnston, while McClair dropped back to feature as the spearhead in midfield. Sitting behind him, a central two were Nicol, who had moved in from the left, and McStay.

Scotland struck again on 63 minutes after Gary Gillespie went on a mazy run on the left and cut inside the penalty area. He rode a couple of challenges and fed Gallacher, whose effort was blocked by Bratseth, and the ball fell into the path of Johnston, who struck left-footed high into the roof of the net. It was a typically instinctive finish. Aitken's tough challenge on Osvold then led to a warning from the referee and Roxburgh, fearing that he may pick up a second booking and a red card, decided to replace him with Ian Durrant on 68 minutes. Willie Miller took over the captaincy.

Scotland were protecting their lead, and McLeish and Miller were keeping strikers Fjørtoft and Gøran Sørloth quiet. The visitors might have been comfortable at this stage, but they could not afford to get complacent and knew there was plenty of time for Norway to come back. Since Durrant had come on, McClair had come even deeper, with Nicol working slightly to their left and McStay appearing just behind them. Scotland would look to play their strikers in, and in Gallacher they had someone who could challenge the Norwegian defence for pace. Gallacher and Johnston both moved into the channels, and this front two posed a greater threat to the hosts than in the first half.

Norway carved out a couple of chances late in the second half. Nicol tugged Fjørtoft back just outside the area and from the ensuing free kick Osvold hit the wall and the ball was scrambled clear. A couple of minutes later, they went closer as captain Anders Giske headed just wide of Leighton's post. Right at the death Jahn Ivar Jakobsen fired wide from a tight angle. Italian referee Agnolin then blew his whistle and the Scottish players celebrated a 2-1 victory and two massive points from a tough away fixture.

6

Yugoslavia Stalemate

19 October 1988 – Scotland 1 Yugoslavia 1

SCOTLAND WELCOMED Yugoslavia to Hampden, the team that Andy Roxburgh regarded as the strongest in Group 5. Led by Ivica Osim, the skilful Eastern Europeans had Red Star Belgrade playmaker Dragan Stojković in midfield and were expected to pose a stern threat.

The last time the two sides met, Scotland had won a friendly 6-1 at Hampden in 1984. Yugoslavia had failed to qualify for the 1986 World Cup and Euro 88 so were determined to make the 1990 finals in Italy.

Roxburgh was dealt a blow when Jim Leighton suffered an injury and had to pull out of the squad, so Andy Goram of Hibernian came in for his fifth cap. Willie Miller captained the side. Richard Gough returned at right-back and Jim Bett earned his 20th cap. Brian McClair and Mo Johnston were retained up front. A crowd of 42,000 saw the Scots line up:

Goram
Gough–Miller (c)–McLeish–Malpas
Nicol–Aitken (Speedie 70)–McStay–Bett (McCoist 55)
Johnston–McClair

The early sequences indicated what was at stake. Neither side appeared willing to relinquish any initiative and there were some ferocious battles for possession. Both teams seemed quite direct; Scotland were not afraid of hoisting long balls forward, where Johnston was working the channels, while the Yugoslavs favoured quick breaks involving several players.

There were a few early set pieces, with Scotland having a right-wing corner and a free kick, while the visitors forced three corners in relatively quick succession. Yugoslavia had several physical players in their side, and were up for the midfield battle. On ten minutes came the first chance for the hosts. McClair spotted Nicol, having made a run in behind defender Predrag Spasić. His shot was saved down to his right by Tomislav Ivković.

The battle for control in midfield was intense, and the general level of close control among the visiting players superb. All over the pitch they had players capable of escaping with the ball even in tight situations. That is what made them such a formidable opponent. They combined individual skill with physical strength, but Scotland continued attempting to play their football.

On 17 minutes Scotland took the lead. Alex McLeish fed Jim Bett who managed to escape the attention of Vujadin Stanojković and fed Maurice Malpas surging forward. He rode a lunge from Srečko Katanec and played a one-two with McClair. The left-back's shot was parried out by Ivković, and striker Johnston reacted the quickest to the rebound, reaching the ball just ahead of Spasić to prod home in off the post. Hampden celebrated the Nantes striker's second goal in two qualifiers.

Yugoslavia kept plugging away, calm in possession, moving the ball about with purpose. Captain Zlatko

Vujović was obstructed by Gough, and the referee awarded the visitors a free kick 25 yards out. Stojković had a go and Goram tipped the ball on to the outside of the post. The subsequent corner brought the equaliser; McStay failed to clear on the near post and midfielder Katanec prodded the ball home. Two minutes later the ball broke Spasić but he fired over from inside the box. A few minutes before the break Nicol's cross picked out Aitken, who had arrived at the back post. With Ivković caught out of position, Aitken's header missed the target. It was 1-1 at half-time.

At the start of the second the two Scottish wide players swapped sides. Steve Nicol had an active first half along the right, where he had combined well with Richard Gough and Mo Johnston to cause trouble to the visitors, whereas Jim Bett had hardly had a sniff along the opposite flank. Nicol's move over to the left brought him closer to the instrumental Stojković as Roxburgh looked to reduce the visitors' attacking strength.

Yugoslavia bossed the first ten minutes of the second half, and Scotland struggled to wrestle free from their grip in midfield. Paul McStay was having an excellent game, always probing and looking for the forward pass. At the back, Alex McLeish was outstanding. Ally McCoist replaced Bett on 55 minutes in a substitution that helped Scotland raise their game a little with McClair dropping back into central midfield and McCoist moving up top alongside Johnston.

Yugoslavia carved out another opening with Stanojković shooting over after Stojković's lay-off. Even though both teams seemed unable to carve out any clear openings in the second half, the game had plenty of nerves and tension. Both sides remained totally committed, and no player shirked any challenges. The visitors gave as good as they got and remained solid. For Scotland, Nicol was working well in tandem with Malpas along the left, making it difficult for Stojković to maintain his stranglehold on the game.

With 20 minutes left Scotland made their second substitution, taking off Aitken and replacing him with David Speedie of Coventry. They continued to press forward but Yugoslavia striker Borislav Cvetković broke clear and Goram saved his weak effort. McCoist, who had been involved in an earlier incident with Yugoslavia defender Faruk Hadžibegić, went down inside the penalty area, claiming that he'd been caught by Spasić. The referee waved play on initially, and when the ball went out of play, he booked McCoist for simulation. Replays of the incident showed that the striker attempted to make the most of it, but there did seem to be some contact and Scotland could have been awarded a penalty.

Ten minutes from time came the biggest goalscoring opportunity. Goram's huge goal kick caught in the wind and evaded McCoist and Hadžibegić. Johnston challenged Ljubomir Radanović and the ball broke loose. McCoist connected right-footed first time. Ivković made a tremendous low save, and although the ball popped back out to Johnston he scuffed the rebound straight into the keeper's arms.

The remaining minutes saw Scotland finish stronger. Yugoslavia continued to struggle in clearing their lines when facing high balls into their box. The visitors were fortunate to see an attempted clearance by Hadžibegić that fell straight at the feet of McCoist bouncing in the hands of Ivković. The ball could easily have gone either side of the goalkeeper, but that was the last action and the game ended in a 1-1 draw.

It had been a relatively open first half, in which the hosts battled well. There had been a good pace to the game. Yugoslavia had probably been slightly the more dominant team, though there had been few saves for Goram to make. After the break, Scotland gained back some momentum and once Bett had been withdrawn for McCoist, they appeared to be a greater threat. It had been a good game and a great contest, always intense. A draw was a fair result.

22 December 1988 – Italy 2 Scotland 0

Surprisingly, Scotland did not play a friendly in November but Roxburgh wanted another game against tough opposition, so on 22 December they went to Perugia to play against Italy.

In a low-key game in front of 25,000 fans they lined up as follows:

Goram
Gough (Speedie 87)–Narey–McLeish
Malpas–Aitken (c)–McStay (McClair 56)–Ferguson
(Durie 71)–MacLeod
Johnston–Gallacher

There was a minute's silence in memory of the victims of the Lockerbie air disaster the day before. Italy started well and kept passion in midfield. Gianluca Vialli fired straight at Goram from a corner, then at the other end Roy Aitken forced a good save from Walter Zenga on 14 minutes. Italy fought back and Giuseppe Giannini was so unlucky when he chipped Goram only to see the ball hit the angle of post and crossbar. The keeper denied him again just before the interval as the first half ended goalless.

In the 49th minute Italy were awarded a soft penalty with the French referee, Alain Delmer, deciding that Gough had impeded Aldo Serena, and Giannini beat Goram from the spot. Brian McClair replaced Paul McStay on 56 minutes. He made a fine run past Franco Baresi to set up Kevin Gallacher who fired wide.

Ian Ferguson of Rangers was having an impressive debut and Scotland felt they should have been awarded a penalty when Gallacher was caught by a high boot from Baresi in the area, then later Mo Johnston felt he was manhandled by Ferrara, but Delmer waved away both appeals.

On 71 minutes Goram made an excellent save from Massimo Crippa's header but Nicola Berti headed home the rebound. Neither Johnston nor Gallacher could find any space against a massed Italian defence, with the outstanding Baresi and Paolo Maldini in imperious form. On 76 minutes Gordon Durie replaced Ferguson with Gallacher moving to the right. However, it was Italy who almost added a third when Goram had to be alert to save from Crippa at his near post. David Speedie replaced Richard Gough in the last few minutes before Alex McLeish headed a free kick into Stefano Tacconi's arms and at full time Italy were comfortable winners.

It was a sobering defeat but Roxburgh had tried a new system and given Ferguson a debut. He had also tried Dortmund's Murdo MacLeod on the left and gave Gordon Durie a run-out in the closing stages. The game underlined the deficiencies in midfield with Roy Aitken often being outrun and outpowered by younger, skilful players. The defence was solid enough with Goram sound and capable and Gough had looked comfortable at centre-back, his preferred position, with David Narey making a notable return to the team. Considering the number of players unavailable, it was a fairly decent performance, but Roxburgh knew his players would have to raise their game against Cyprus in February.

7

Cyprus Chaos

8 February 1989 – Cyprus 2 Scotland 3

ANDY ROXBURGH knew that this game could be a potential banana skin. Cyprus had held France to a 1-1 draw in October, a shock result that had badly damaged Michel Platini's team's chances of qualifying for the World Cup.

The match was shown live on STV with commentary from Jock Brown and Alex Ferguson.

The majority of Scots in the 25,000 crowd were expats living on the island but a few hundred of the Tartan Army made the trip. Among them were Julie and Ian Simpson from Dundee. Julie explained, 'We had planned the trip a few months before as my brother Tom lived in Cyprus. So we managed to get a cheap flight and there were a few hundred of us in the ground. Given our record against weaker teams we knew it was going to be a long hard afternoon. Little did we know what drama was to come!'

On a warm afternoon on a poor and bumpy pitch, Roxburgh opted for an experienced team:

Leighton
Gough–Narey–McLeish–Malpas
Nicol (Ferguson 9)–Aitken (c)–McStay–McClair
Johnston–Speedie (McInally 68)

Cyprus had earned a famous 1-1 draw at home to France in their opening qualifier. In their next home game, against Norway in November, they started brightly. They were aggressive, put the Norwegians under severe first-half pressure and they'd managed to create openings, even if they had not been able to tuck any of them away. Norway would eventually run out 3-0 winners. Scotland would've been expecting a similar tough test, but the visitors were well prepared. They kept a good shape early on and they went in front from their very first chance on nine minutes. The strike came courtesy of Mo Johnston's third goal in the qualification, and the flame-haired 24-year-old, in his 24th appearance for his country, stole in to capitalise on a poor header back by Cyprus midfielder Pavlos Savva. His header sent Johnston racing away and Makis Socratous was unable to stop him on the edge of the penalty area. Johnston fired the ball on the half-volley past goalkeeper Giorgos Pantziaras to give the Scots a 1-0 lead. It was his ninth goal for his country.

Almost immediately, there was a substitution by the visitors, as Steve Nicol, suffering from food poisoning, was replaced by young Rangers man Ian Ferguson. Ferguson, wearing number 13, slotted directly into the position left by Nicol on the right side of midfield.

Since an early effort by Giorgos Savvidis, there had not been any threat towards Jim Leighton's goal. Scotland seemed well in control, and Roy Aitken's effort from 30 yards flew over the bar. A few minutes later the ball was in the back of the Scottish net courtesy of Cyprus wide man Christos Koliantris. While Scotland had been gifted their goal by Savva, it was the hosts' turn to capitalise on some shoddy defending. Floros Nicolaou lifted a ball through to the edge of the area, where Koliantris put pressure on David Narey, who still seemed to be in control of the situation. However, as the ball bounced high off the dry pitch, Narey's attempted clearance bounced off the chasing Koliantris and fell kindly, for him to calmly slot past Leighton for the equaliser.

The game was not a high-quality affair. Cyprus seemed pleased with the slow pace, which meant they were able to compete with their opponents. Indeed, they were the ones drawing the next save from either goalkeeper, when their talismanic captain Yiannakis Yiangoudakis managed to squeeze a shot through the legs of Alex McLeish from inside the penalty area, but his effort lacked conviction and Leighton claimed the ball.

It was at times scrappy, which could be partly blamed on conditions. The wind appeared to be blowing in patches, and the pitch was poor, which meant that the ball kept bouncing awkwardly. Scotland were quite direct and aimed passes long in the direction of their two strikers, Johnston and David Speedie. They did have good footballers in the centre of the park, but neither Paul McStay nor substitute Ferguson were allowed much time to keep possession. Ferguson did well whenever he could take an extra touch or two, and he seemed quite confident despite this just being his second international.

Cyprus, on the other hand, were best described as plucky. They were certainly not afraid of going to ground claiming injury. It had happened several times early in the match, and they used those tactics more frequently as the 90 minutes progressed. They did have some players who were quite capable in possession, but collectively they were not strong enough to put Scotland under any sustained level of pressure and they had not been able to really test Leighton.

Scotland ended the first half on a strong note as they probably took advantage of some weariness among the hosts. Ferguson continued his midfield promise, and it was when he and McStay combined that the Scots looked to be at their best. Aitken swung a cross towards the back post, where the marauding Richard Gough met it, but he failed to get sufficient power behind his header, which was comfortably held by Pantziaras. It was 1-1 at the interval.

Just over two minutes into the second half Cyprus went ahead. Leighton failed to hold a free kick into the area from left-back Charalambos Pittas, and Maurice Malpas hoofed it out for a corner. Savvidis swung it into the centre of the six-yard box, Leighton again failed to claim it as he flapped at it, and when the ball fell loose in the area, several home players tried to get shots away, until it worked its way out to midfielder Nicolaou at the right side of the area.

His low cross-cum-shot was turned home on the far post by Yiannos Ioannou for a second Cypriot goal of the afternoon. The goal was Ioannou's second for his country, and the 25,000-strong crowd erupted, eyeing another upset.

How would Scotland respond to that shock second goal? They kept knocking the ball forward quickly and right-back Gough hit a low shot from an angle into the side netting without troubling Pantziaras. Cyprus almost increased their lead when Ioannou squared the ball for his two team-mates in front of goal. Unfortunately for the hosts, his low cross from the left had too much pace, Savvidis and Koliantris both failing to connect, and Malpas scrambled clear.

While the first half had been watchable, if not with a whole lot of quality in it, the start to the second half was frantic. Scotland refused to panic and they continued to look for openings. There was a notable change in their midfield dynamic, though, as Ferguson moved across from the right to the left. Brian McClair then went the other way.

On 54 minutes Gough, who had already had three goal attempts, levelled the score. He had stayed up after a McClair throw from the right, which was headed on by McStay into the path of Speedie. He managed to get in behind his marker Giorgos Christodoulou and hooked it back for Johnston. He laid it off for Gough to fire home and make it 2-2; Cyprus's lead had lasted for just seven minutes. Scotland were invigorated by Gough's goal, his fourth for his country in 41 appearances, and Speedie enjoyed his best spell of the game. The little striker had often struggled in battle with Christodoulou, and he had a firm header from just inside the area saved by Pantziaras following an Aitken free kick.

McClair almost gifted the hosts a third goal when he failed to look up and see Savvidis as he played the ball back to Leighton. Luckily for the Manchester United striker, Savvidis somehow failed to control it and Leighton gratefully pounced on the ball.

Roxburgh decided to make a second substitution on 68 minutes, taking off Speedie and bringing on Aston Villa striker Alan McInally. Speedie had been hobbling around after a stiff challenge. For the physically imposing 25-year-old McInally, it was his debut at international level. He was having a fine season in the English top flight, and with Roxburgh opting for a target man rather than the more dynamic Kevin Gallacher, he felt that they needed someone to impose an aerial threat to the Cypriot defence.

Scotland lacked quality in their final pass, and so were unable to make further inroads on the Cypriot goal. The match was still evenly balanced as the clock ticked into the last 15 minutes. McInally had initially shown some strength as he appeared to bulldoze his way forward when tracked by Pittas out on Scotland's right but, that incident apart, he had been unable to make a big impression. Mo Johnston was anonymous too, trying to feed off scraps and little service.

It became increasingly evident that Cyprus were content with a point, and they made little effort in sending men forward in search of further goals. There was another piece of theatrics when goalkeeper Pantziaras went down after a very faint touch from McInally, and the 36-year-old made the most of it, prompting Gough to remind the referee to add extra time for it.

In a moment of sheer brilliance, Johnston came close to adding to his tally ten minutes from time. From a very deep right-wing corner from McStay, Johnston outside the penalty area, slightly to the left, he struck a half-volley which cannoned off the underside of Pantziaras's crossbar, almost by the angle with the post. The Nantes striker was desperately unlucky to not see it find the back of the net. As Scotland still searched desperately for that elusive third goal they continued to apply the pressure, while the clock must have been ticking down slowly for the hosts, who just seemed interested in seeing time out. They took every opportunity at set pieces to slow proceedings down, and they were certainly not afraid to go down to waste more time.

There was a great deal of urgency to the Scottish game, although they were still unable to penetrate the hosts with the clock going past 90 minutes. They kept looking for second balls off McInally but Cyprus defended for their lives, booting or heading the ball anywhere, away from goal. They had strength in numbers, and they didn't mind conceding corners as long as it got the ball out of harm's way. Gough arrived to head a McStay corner well wide in what was a big chance.

On 94 minutes Socratous booted the ball into touch inside the Scotland half and no ball boy went to assist the visitors in retrieving it. Scotland played on and won a free kick in a promising position down the left, when Ferguson was impeded by Nicolaou. Captain Aitken swung one final ball into the penalty area and Gough powered in a header for the winner. The clock showed 95 minutes and 32 seconds as the ball went into the back of the net, and the Scots had their precious third goal. Such late drama, and home players and fans couldn't believe it. The visiting players celebrated like they had won the World Cup. All of Cyprus's time-wasting had come back to haunt them. Time was up with Scotland in possession inside their own half. They had come back from the dead and turned the game around for what could potentially prove to be a hugely important 3-2 victory.

Some Cypriot fans were furious that the referee had added six minutes of injury time, something which was almost unheard of at the time. After the final whistle they felt provoked into action, and they took to the pitch to confront the referee, Siegfried Kirschen, and the Scottish team. There were claims that Kirschen was punched, and riot police would be needed to make sure of his and the Scottish team's safety. It would take Kirschen and his assistants half an hour to leave the pitch. Ugly, unsavoury scenes. Ultimately, the Cypriot FA would receive a fine from FIFA, and they would have to play their one remaining home qualifier outside of the country.

Scotland had snatched an unlikely victory. Jim Leighton had looked shaky and David Narey would never play for Scotland again. It was hard to explain why they fell behind and why they created so little. The midfield balance still seemed wrong, not helped by Nicol's injury. Mo Johnston had scored his third goal in three qualifiers and that was encouraging.

Scotland had got out of jail, and a relieved Andy Roxburgh told the *Daily Record*, 'It was a very difficult game. They are a decent side and gave us problems. We lost two bad goals and the pitch was terrible. We knew the Cypriots liked to waste time, it was incredible really. The ball boys did not return the ball and they wasted time taking corners, throws and free kicks. The referee only added the time on because their players were rolling around pretending to be injured. Not many would have played so much injury time so credit to the referee for being strong enough.

'Richard Gough scored two great goals and we got two priceless points. We can play much better but the win is all that matters.'

The *Glasgow Evening Times* reported, 'The Swiss precision of a stopwatch couldn't camouflage the frailties, but Gough's leap from Aitken's cross was classic.'

The *Glasgow Herald* headline was 'Scots Victory Provokes Riot', which was followed by 'Fans suffer as Scots flirt with lasting shame'.

Years later Gough told Archie Macpherson in his book, *Adventures in the Golden Age: Scotland at The World Cup*

Finals 1974–1998, 'I thought big Roy was a great player, but always felt that his best position was central defender and not the kind of holding midfield position he played for Scotland. But the great thing about him is he never gave up. Neither would I. I have to say when his cross came over, my header for the winner was one of the best I had ever made. The right jump, right contact. I knew then we had made it.'

For expat couple Brenda and Simon Forsyth the game was a rare chance to see Scotland play. Brenda recalled, 'We had retired in 1987 and had fallen in love with Cyprus ever since our honeymoon in the 1970s. We knew a few families over here and there was quite a large community of British people. We are both Partick Thistle fans and although we had been to a few England games at Hampden, we hadn't really been to many Scotland games. We managed to get a cheap pair of tickets through my old boss and thought it might be a good game to go to. It was awful! We were all over the place at the back and when Gough scored in injury time, all hell broke loose. Coins were thrown on to the pitch, bottles and even a firework. We were just glad to get out in one piece.'

Simon added, 'It was a strange game on a poor pitch. Narey was awful and Leighton kept flapping at cross balls. We got out of jail really. When we went 2-1 down I feared the worst but it was a massive win in the end. Gough's late header was immense. It all got a bit crazy at full time so we were glad to get out of there.'

Mo's French Fireworks

8 March 1989 – Scotland 2 France 0

FRANCE HAD had a slow start to their campaign, and were still lagging behind after that shock draw in Cyprus. Michel Platini had come in as manager and this was his second qualifier in charge. *Les Bleus* had not played since November, but had prepared themselves for this game with a 0-0 friendly draw against the Republic of Ireland in February.

As usual, Andy Roxburgh had planned meticulously. He knew everything about France, had seen them play many times, watched videos and read match reports. Mo Johnston, now playing for Nantes, also provided information on the French defenders.

It was the biggest game in Roxburgh's career so far and he had spent three years building up a side for this moment. There was, however, one thing he could not plan for – the Glasgow traffic! The coach got stuck in a jam and panic started to set in. It was just an hour before kick-off but they were still not moving. Luckily, Roy Aitken had one of the first brick-sized mobile phones. He was able to call the police, who gave them a police escort to Hampden. The players arrived just half an hour before the start of the match.

Roxburgh chose the standard 4-4-2 formation with no real surprises in the team selection. Johnston was first choice as striker, but who would partner him? Scotland had started their qualifying campaign for Italia 90 with Brian McClair alongside Johnston, but he had delivered some average performances so far. Ally McCoist had only just returned from injury and was given the nod ahead of the Manchester United man.

The most troublesome position in the Scottish team, however, was the left side of midfield, where Roxburgh had tried out various players with little success. Ian Ferguson had made a decent impression as an early sub against Cyprus, and he was given another chance here.

Another player returning from injury was Gary Gillespie, who had played just one qualifier so far, away against Norway. He had given a man-of-the-match performance at right-back, but with Richard Gough back in that position, Gillespie slotted in at centre-back alongside Alex McLeish.

Platini picked virtually the same team that featured in the friendly against the Republic of Ireland and went for a 5-3-2 formation. France had also played an unofficial friendly against Arsenal too, losing 2-0 at Highbury on 14 February. The most important change in selection was the introduction of uncapped Sochaux midfielder Thierry Laurey. He joined midfielders Laurent Blanc and Jean-Philippe Durand, who did not have much experience at international level, having in total amassed four caps before this evening. Fielding Laurey in midfield, Platini pushed Franck Sauzée to the right wing-back position.

The midfield was relatively untested at this level, but there was experience through Patrick Battiston, who had been tempted out of international retirement by Platini. He would play as a libero between the two man-markers. There was also a place in the line-up for Franck Silvestre, who had earned his first cap against Ireland and had done well in keeping Tony Cascarino quiet. He would be a man-marker here in the absence of Basile Boli, who was banned after picking up two yellow cards in the qualification so far. Jean Tigana had been selected for the squad, but had to pull out through injury.

Scotland lined up with:

Leighton
Gough–Gillespie–McLeish (c)–Malpas
Nicol–Aitken–McStay–Ferguson (Strachan 56)
Johnston–McCoist (McClair 69)

Over 65,000 filled the Hampden terraces for a clash between two different styles of football: Scotland with their sometimes more direct approach and France with their possession play through midfield. The key battles would be between the two Scottish strikers and the two French man-markers: McCoist v Silvestre and Johnston v Luc Sonor.

Roxburgh's tactical instructions were to bypass the midfield and play direct balls forward in the direction of McCoist and Johnston. Scotland would otherwise have found it difficult to make transitions from midfield to attack. The central midfield was congested with France having a surplus player and Steve Nicol sometimes dropping in alongside Aitken and McStay when the visitors were on the ball.

McCoist and Johnston proved to be excellent focal points for Scotland's build-up play and were instrumental as the home side managed to retain long spells of pressure from the beginning of the match. The two forwards worked tirelessly to free themselves from their markers and by dropping deep to collect the ball they were successful in bringing the midfielders into play.

In this way, it didn't matter if Scotland were in inferior numbers in central midfield or if there were questions about their quality in the wide areas. The direct approach was sufficient to establish play high up the field and make sure Scotland were on top of the game.

More important than the two forwards' ability to hold up the ball, however, was the recklessness of Sonor and Silvestre. The two markers were persistently fouling McCoist and Johnston as they continued diving into tackles. They may have been instructed to tackle hard, but here it bordered on the ridiculous at times, as it almost appeared that they couldn't get into a tussle with the forwards without committing a foul. The cost of this aggressive tackling was that Scotland were given a plethora of free kicks, which were among their main weapons.

Scotland continued to hoist the ball in the direction of Richard Gough, whose reputation for towering headers was growing by the day. His two goals against Cyprus the previous month had both been from set pieces. The number of free kicks ensured that Scotland could move players forward and establish a presence in the final third, while France struggled to find their own tempo on the ball.

Not unsurprisingly, it was through a set piece that Scotland would score the opening goal. This time it was, however, not a free kick prompted by a foul on McCoist or Johnston but a minor offence committed by Daniel Xuereb on Gillespie just beyond the halfway line. Gough couldn't connect with the ball as it was hoisted in his direction, but McCoist picked it up and fired a tame shot that turned out to be an excellent pass to Johnston, who found himself one-on-one with French goalkeeper Joël Bats. Johnston had been left unattended in the melee, and calmly slotted his shot past Bats. It was Johnston's fourth goal of the Italia 90 campaign, making him the top scorer of the UEFA qualification zone so far.

As against Yugoslavia away in a 3-2 defeat in November, France played with three central midfielders, with Platini wanting to dominate play in midfield and play through the middle. In theory, Platini had a strong central line here that was designed to move the ball from defence to attack, with Battiston linking defence and midfield, and Xuereb connecting midfield and attack. The idea was for these players to combine their way forward by overloading Scotland in the middle.

The big question here was the unproven midfield trio, who had almost no experience at this level. Their inexperience did perhaps also show, as it took considerable time before France managed to establish any play in the middle. They seemed intimidated by Scotland's high tempo on the ball, unable to dictate proceedings themselves. Gradually, however, and more and more so after going a goal down, France started to impose themselves by taking advantage of their strong central spine. Battiston played some incisive forward passes, Xuereb did well to lay the ball off and the three central midfielders at times ran over the Scottish midfield, as they always seemed to be getting themselves into space. Some of the best attacking moves were produced by France, although they rarely managed to get behind the Scottish defence, and were restricted to long shots.

Wing-backs are usually vital in a 5-3-2 system, but the attacking contributions from Manuel Amoros and Sauzée were few and far between. Amoros did manage to get into the Scottish half at times. He battled his way forward with the ball at his feet, but he rarely knew what to do once high up the pitch. Sauzée appeared to be cautious because of the presence of Ian Ferguson, and perhaps also uncomfortable in his new position. The lack of support from the wing-backs was also in stark contrast to the game in Belgrade, where the 4-3-3 formation ensured that France were threatening in the wide areas throughout.

There were no changes at half-time, and the second half unfolded in the same pattern. Scotland doubled their lead eight minutes after the break and again it was Johnston on target. Again it was not very pretty, but efficient football from the Scots. The attack had only been instigated by a pass simply being hoisted forward from Richard Gough from the deep of his right-back position. Sonor's clumsy attempt to control the loose ball was pounced on by the tireless McCoist, who regained possession near the byline.

McCoist set up Nicol to swing in a beautiful cross aimed in the space between Bats and the defence, which Johnston was the first to connect with. Bats first parried Johnston's header, but then fumbled the ball over the goal line to make it 2-0.

Roxburgh made a change shortly after the goal, replacing Ferguson with Gordon Strachan in the 56th minute. Strachan took his usual position wide on the right, prompting a switch for the versatile Nicol from right to left. Ferguson was not a natural wide player, and did seem to be a bit lost for ideas when advancing down the left with the ball at feet. He seemed more comfortable the times that he drifted inside.

Nicol, however, was having a great game. His tenacity and work rate made the most out of whatever position he was asked to play in, and he produced some powerful running at Amoros. He probably had more success as a right-sided midfielder this evening than after switching to the opposite side, but Scotland were also less intent on attacking once going 2-0 up.

There was half an hour left to stage a comeback, but France never managed to find the goal that could bring them back into the game. They did have the occasional chance, mainly through Jean-Pierre Papin, but he was denied by Jim Leighton, who made three great saves in one of his best appearances for Scotland. The central defence in front of him was excellent too, instrumental in denting the many attacking movements that sprung from the French midfield. Scotland saw out the rest of the game for a famous 2-0 win.

Scotland were on top from the start and got the important first goal. The tireless McCoist and Johnston were instrumental in everything they did, and Johnston scored two goals, bringing his total to five so far in the qualification.

It was a rousing win and a great performance, on one of Hampden's greatest nights. Roxburgh was delighted and post-match told ITV's Brian Moore, 'I am very pleased. We needed a big performance and I thought the boys were magnificent. Mo will get all the headlines but it was a great all-round team performance. Jim Leighton was outstanding and we defended well when we had to and were always a threat.'

9

Scotland Mo-mentum

26 April 1989 – Scotland 2 Cyprus 1

WITH THE summer looming, Scotland were looking to further consolidate their position at the top of Group 5. Their start with seven points from a possible eight had brought plenty of optimism and, with a home fixture against expected whipping boys Cyprus next up, even the most pessimistic supporters must have been eyeing another two points. This was the Scots' third qualifier within the space of two and a half months, and having overcome Cyprus away and France at home, they were big favourites to maintain their stronghold on the group. Andy Roxburgh had so far made use of 21 players, with the inclusion of experienced winger Gordon Strachan as a substitute against the French. Strachan had since made an eyebrow-raising move from Manchester United to arch rivals Leeds United, who were playing in the Second Division. He was not included in Roxburgh's squad of 16 for this clash.

With this game taking place 11 days after the Hillsborough tragedy in England, where more than 90 Liverpool fans had perished at the club's FA Cup semi-final meeting with Nottingham Forest at Sheffield Wednesday's stadium, none of the two Liverpool players who had been picked for the game would be taking part. It was likely that central defender Gary Gillespie would have partnered Alex McLeish but he was out with an injury and had not featured at club level since early April. Steve Nicol, an ever-present for Liverpool during the 1988/89 season, pulled out of the squad, like his team-mates John Barnes (England) and John Aldridge (Republic of Ireland) had done for matches on this same date.

A third player who had been in the starting 11 in the victory over France, Rangers' young midfield man Ian Ferguson, was also not in the squad. Add to those Brian McClair of Manchester United and the already mentioned Strachan, there was a total of five changes since their last matchday squad. Coming into the squad for a possible debut was Dave McPherson, a 25-year-old from Hearts, along with Everton's tricky winger Pat Nevin and Aberdeen's prolific forward Charlie Nicholas, with six and 19 former caps respectively, in addition to Dundee United's trusted midfielder Jim McInally (three caps) and Chelsea striker Gordon Durie (capped twice).

Knowing what was demanded of them, nothing but a win, Scotland had picked plenty of attacking power. There were six recognised forwards in Mo Johnston, Ally McCoist, David Speedie, Kevin Gallacher, Durie and Nicholas. With so many strikers, would Roxburgh pick a more attacking formation this time around? They had flirted with three centre-backs during the winter, when they'd played Italy away and lost 2-0 in a December friendly. In their four qualifiers since, though, 4-4-2 had been the order of the day.

Leighton
Gough–McPherson–McLeish–Malpas
Nevin (Nicholas 74)–Aitken (c)–McStay–Durie
(Speedie 59)
Johnston–McCoist

The Hampden stands were packed with over 50,000 fans for a game against lowly opponents, which showed the enthusiasm for Roxburgh's men. McCoist and Paul McStay got the game under way. For the hosts, there was a debut at the back as McPherson got the nod and became Alex McLeish's fourth different partner since the start of qualification, with Willie Miller, David Narey and Gary Gillespie all having already featured alongside him. McLeish had carried the captain's armband against France, but it was returned to midfielder Roy Aitken.

In goal, there was another appearance for Manchester United's Jim Leighton. This was his fourth game of the qualification campaign, with the home fixture against Yugoslavia the only one that he'd missed out on. There were also familiar faces at both full-back positions, with the marauding Richard Gough to Leighton's right and Dundee United's two-footed stalwart Maurice Malpas playing to the left. Gough had been a big thorn in Cyprus's side last time the two countries had met, with those two goals, including that injury-time winner, from a total of six attempts. Could he exert the same level of attacking influence once again?

Despite fielding a flurry of strikers in their 16-man matchday squad, Scotland were in a familiar 4-4-2 from the off. Their midfield consisted of Aitken alongside his Celtic team-mate McStay in the centre, just like in their four previous qualifiers. McStay had probably been their best player altogether so far, with some appearances being of the highest calibre. He was busy, able to perform a high level of pressing, skilful in possession, had a fair shot and was usually their go-to man for central creativity.

McStay was capable of opening up an opponent's defence with intelligent passing, and already at the age of 24 he had clocked up 36 internationals. The Aitken-McStay combination appeared a good fit also at international level, with the former often doing the less visible dirty work just behind his colleague.

In Pat Nevin, Scotland also had probably one of the game's few out-and-out wingers. As is the case with most wide players, they were often either on or off their game. An on-song Nevin could be a major asset, and Roxburgh hoped he would bring threat and balance on the right. It was the former Chelsea man's first involvement since their failed qualification campaign ahead of Euro 88. On the left was Gordon Durie, Nevin's former team-mate in west London. It was Durie's first appearance during the qualifiers, and was only the 23-year-old striker's third cap for his country.

Just as against France, Roxburgh opted for the forward combination of Johnston and McCoist. The former had been in prolific form so far, and his two goals against France had taken him up to five from four qualifiers. McCoist, so prolific with Rangers, was making his 15th appearance for his country, although he had yet to open his account in the qualifiers so far.

The first signs of danger came when Durie was played in along the left and cut inside and fired a right-footed shot about 20 yards out. His effort had pace but not the direction to trouble the Cypriot goalkeeper Andreas Charitou, and it flew a few yards wide of the upright. Next, he won a left-wing corner off Makis Socratous. He took the kick himself, which sailed towards the far post, and Charitou palmed it away. Coming in at the far post, McCoist hammered a shot goalwards. Although Cyprus had several defenders between the striker and the goal line, and it was an acute angle, Charitou parried the shot. The Scots recycled the ball and set up McPherson for a header which drifted wide.

On 26 minutes came the opening goal, which was a brilliant overhead kick by the red-hot Johnston. The Cypriot defence struggled to clear their lines, and when Nevin was allowed to cross for a second time in the same move, the little winger found Gough at the far post. The right-back headed it back into the centre, where Giorgos Christodoulou made a mess of his clearance, and the ball sat up for Johnston, with a chance to perform a spectacular overhead kick. He connected sweetly, with Charitou left with no chance to stop the ball from whistling into the back of the net. It was a sensational goal, out of nothing, with Mo at his opportunist best.

The hosts were constantly finding their wide players and firing crosses into the box. Nevin had played his part in the opening goal, but Durie had also been well involved so far, and he again crossed from the left towards the back post. Charitou, who seemed to struggle in dealing with high balls, again flapped at it, this time challenged by Johnston. The ball was kept in play by Charalambos Pittas, but he could not get any conviction behind his attempted clearance. Nevin again crossed from the right and Johnston in the centre managed to get his head to the ball but it drifted harmlessly wide.

Towards the end of the first half, there was almost an own goal from defender Christodoulou, as he headed another teasing Durie cross from the left against his own post. It was very clumsy from the big centre-back, and he was fortunate that the ball cannoned off the upright rather than ending up in the back of his own net. Johnston's goal separated the sides at half-time.

ITV commentator Brian Moore noted that Johnston had equalled the national record of seven World Cup goals in qualifiers and tournaments proper, shared by Kenny Dalglish and Joe Jordan, with his spectacular strike.

Just past the hour Gough fouled lone Cyprus striker Giorgos Savvidis out by the touchline. It was a cheap foul as Savvidis was going nowhere and away from goal. Even if he'd made it past the big defender, his lack of pace would probably have seen him caught before he could get into a crossing position. Scotland had McPherson covering behind Gough.

Up stepped left-back Pittas to swing one into the area with his left foot. His cross was met by Floros Nicolaou some ten yards out from goal, and with a static Malpas caught ball watching, the defensive midfielder was able to get a deft touch to it ahead of the left-back, and was able to guide the ball superbly into the back of the net with a looping effort. Leighton had expected a cross towards the far post and had come off his goal line but was left stranded as the ball sailed over his head for a stunning equaliser.

A few minutes before the goal, there had been a first substitution of the game, as Roxburgh withdrew the lively Durie and replaced him with another former Chelsea team-mate of his, now at Coventry, David Speedie, with the striker slotting directly into the left of midfield.

The Scottish players reacted straight away and instead of sulking over the equaliser they fought back. From the kick-off they were back on the attack and they were rewarded with a second goal just one minute after the leveller. The ball was worked out to the right wing where Nevin won a throw-in off Pittas. McStay threw short to Nevin, who held Costas Petsas off before feeding it back to McStay. The midfielder sidestepped a challenge from the onrushing Savvidis and then took the ball between Petsas and Socratous, before making it to the byline. He fired in a low cross for McCoist, who arrived just ahead of his marker Spyros Kastanas to side-foot the ball into the back of the net. It was quality play by McStay, and Scotland had hit back instantly for a 2-1 lead.

Cyprus were offering nothing going forward and McCoist's cross-cum-shot almost found Speedie at the far post. However, the substitute just failed to reach it, and the ball ran out of play. Roxburgh made a second substitution on 74 minutes, Nevin being replaced by Charlie Nicholas.

Soon after, right-back Gough arrived on the far side of the area to get his head to a deep Johnston cross from the left. Charitou had started to come for the ball, then realised he would not get there and took a step back, and was in no-man's land. Fortunately for him, Gough could not direct his looping header on target, seeing the ball go agonisingly wide of the left-hand post, with McCoist unable to get a touch. Another left-wing cross, this time from captain Aitken, towards the back post, was met by Johnston but luckily for the visitors, and especially their flappy goalkeeper, Christodoulou was on hand to head it off the line. Despite more late pressure, there were no more goals and at full time Scotland had won 2-1.

Scotland deserved their two points, even if they made hard work of it. They were now sitting four points clear at the top of the table, albeit having played two games more than the fancied Yugoslavs. It was a more comfortable victory than the final scoreline suggested as Cyprus scored with their first shot on target. Pat Nevin made a notable return to the team, providing width and creativity from the right. Mo Johnston had now scored six times in qualifiers and his overhead kick was one of the best goals seen at Hampden for many years.

Scotland had nine points out of a possible ten and were on the brink of qualification for their fifth World Cup in a row. For Andy Roxburgh and his assistant Craig Brown it was the culmination of years of hard work, preparation and tactical awareness. They were blessed with some excellent players who were playing with confidence and with the Tartan Army right behind them.

Roxburgh told the *Daily Record*, 'I am pleased with the result although they gave us a scare when they scored. Thankfully, we hit back straight away. I thought Pat Nevin did well and what can you say about Mo Johnston? A world-class strike. We are almost there now.'

10

1989 Rous Cup

26 May 1989 – Scotland 0 England 2

THIS WAS the second game of the 1989 edition of Rous Cup, a mini-tournament that by now was running for a fifth successive year, in the wake of the decision to abandon the British Home Championship after its 1983/84 edition. Originally, it was meant to continue the annual meetings of Scotland and England, although this was the third successive year in which a South American country had been welcomed to take part, making it a three-team tournament. It would turn out to be the last Rous Cup ever staged.

While Brazil, the 1987 winners, and Colombia had taken part in the two previous editions, Chile had this time been invited to keep the two home nations company. Argentina had originally been asked, but they'd turned down the invitation. Chile had already played out their first game of the tournament, keeping England to a scoreless draw in London four days earlier. It was time for the oldest fixture on the international football calendar to take place again, some 117 years after their inaugural meeting, a 0-0 affair in Glasgow.

It appears unclear exactly how many players had been selected for each nations' tournament squads, but it is likely that five players were allowed on the substitutes' bench, much like in a typical qualifier.

The game took place a week after the Scottish FA Cup Final had played out at Hampden, where Celtic had beaten Rangers 1-0 with Joe Miller the scorer. Four Celtic players were part of the Scotland squad, while Rangers had three, in addition to three also in the England squad. Celtic manager Billy McNeill was one of the people watching from the directors' box.

The Scotland squad of 16 was very different this time due to injuries, although the core of their team remained. On the injured list were players such as midfielders Ian Ferguson and Jim Bett, as well as forwards Charlie Nicholas, Gordon Durie, Kevin Gallacher and also Graeme Sharp, who could possibly have been in contention for a place in the squad. Scotland had even lost influential defender Richard Gough through injury after his call-up, and so Andy Roxburgh had drafted in Aberdeen full-back Stewart McKimmie as a possible replacement. McKimmie, so far uncapped, was rumoured to be unsettled at the east coast club, and could perhaps see this as an opportunity to put himself in the shop window should he get game time.

It was also thought that striker Ally McCoist was carrying a knock, which he had picked up during the Scottish Cup Final. He was being worked on by Scotland and Celtic physio Jimmy Steel, who would eventually declare McCoist fit and available.

The four players coming into the squad since Cyprus were midfielders Peter Grant of Celtic, another possible debutant, Murdo MacLeod of Borussia Dortmund,

Aberdeen's Robert Connor and striker Alan McInally of Aston Villa.

Scotland had played with both four and five men at the back during the last eight or nine months, but their solitary attempt at 5-3-2 had happened only during their 2-0 friendly loss in Italy in December, and so it seemed likely that they would turn out in a 4-4-2 once again.

Four days earlier, England had only managed a goalless draw at home to Chile, in the first match of this tournament, and the following Saturday they were due to face Poland at Wembley in a crucial World Cup qualifier. The annual meeting with Scotland was not something that England would ever take lightly, and they would select a powerful 11 for this Hampden showdown.

England's previous match ahead of the Rous Cup was their 5-0 demolition of Albania at Wembley on 26 April. That had come just 11 days in the wake of the Hillsborough tragedy, something which had meant Liverpool winger John Barnes had not wanted to feature. However, his forward partner at club level, Peter Beardsley, had played against the Albanians, and indeed scored twice. Due to the Liverpool v Arsenal title decider the night before, neither player had been selected for this fixture.

Since the Albania match, five players had left the squad. They were midfielders David Rocastle of Arsenal and Steve Hodge of Nottingham Forest, as well as forwards Beardsley, Gary Lineker of Barcelona and Arsenal's Alan Smith.

Brought into the squad in order to replace the absent players were Everton midfielder Trevor Steven, and a group of forwards including Wimbledon's John Fashanu, who had won his first cap in the 0-0 draw with Chile, Everton's Tony Cottee, Nigel Clough of Nottingham Forest and prolific Wolverhampton Wanderers man Steve Bull, another possible debutant, and potentially only the fifth player from the third tier to win a full England cap. Birthday boy Paul Gascoigne, 22 on the day of the game, kept his place.

England had so far played seven matches in all since the 1988 European Championship, and they'd lined up in a 4-4-2 formation in all of them. Unsurprisingly this wouldn't change for the visit to Glasgow.

This was the 107th clash between Scotland and England. The stats slightly favoured England with 42 wins to Scotland's 40 while 24 matches had ended in draw. They had met once a year since 1947 and even twice in 1973 due to the 100th anniversary of the Scottish FA, but events would unfortunately mean that this was to be the last fixture between the two for seven years due to off-field trouble.

Hooliganism would sadly mar the occasion, with no less than 96 arrests being made inside the stadium and an estimated further 150 outside. This happened even though the English FA had not issued any tickets for English fans, though some away supporters had purchased their tickets through the Scottish FA.

Scotland's line-up was:

Leighton
McKimmie–McPherson–McLeish–Malpas
Nevin–Aitken (c)–McStay–Connor (Grant 58)
Johnston–McCoist

There was always the expectancy that a Scotland v England clash would be fast-paced with a lot of heavy challenges and balls in the air. Duels would be hard but fair. There was almost so much at stake and as a result the games could often be poor spectacles. Their last meeting at Hampden in May 1987 was a tepid 0-0 draw, where two tired teams failed to produce after a long, hard season. It was often stated that the game meant more to the Scots but that was never the case. England players were just as desperate to win as their old rivals.

Once Ally McCoist and Paul McStay had got the ball rolling at kick-off, the crowd would get what they had wanted, which was a battle between two fully committed teams. The media often like to refer to games between big rivals as being 'just like a cup tie' and in this case the expression could be justified. Even if the Rous Cup was hardly the most coveted prize on the international stage, tackling the auld enemy was motivation enough for both sets of players.

Some sections of the English press had claimed in the build-up that Scotland were hardly ideal opponents at the time, considering the importance of the following week's World Cup qualifier against Poland. They'd have wanted to face a more continental team to better prepare to face the Poles, who at the time appeared to be something of an unknown quantity. Poland had lost in Sweden early in the month, but this had only been their second qualifying match.

Scotland, with no qualifier of their own looming imminently, might have felt more relaxed about the fixture, other than the pressure which they'd have put upon themselves. Just as for players in the opposite camp, no Scotland player would want a defeat by England on their CV. However, circumstances made sure that Andy Roxburgh's hands were somewhat tied, with a good few players unavailable to him. Still, they were top of their qualifying group and undefeated, so carrying the momentum into the annual encounter.

The early exchanges showed that the game would be a battle for pride. The pace was high from the word go, and no player seemed to shirk any challenge. With some high-profile English players in the Scottish domestic league, there were bound to be team-mates facing each other directly in battle, and at the heart of the English back line was the towering presence of Terry Butcher, a linchpin in Rangers' defence. With the pace of Nottingham Forest's Des Walker alongside him, they would be a formidable barrier for the Scottish strikers.

Butcher had been part of a defensive unit at the Ibrox club, which had only shipped 26 goals in 36 league matches, and they'd won the title by a margin of six points to second-placed Aberdeen, something which was quite overwhelming considering there were still only two points for a win at that time. Butcher would often lock horns with Rangers team-mate Ally McCoist, a proven goalscorer domestically, but perhaps so far not to the same extent at an international level. He'd notched four times in 15 previous appearances, although he had netted the winner in his most recent feature: the 2-1 win against Cyprus. The Butcher v McCoist duels could prove key to the game.

Wimbledon striker John Fashanu, who had rounded off the domestic season with 12 league goals to his name, had become the very first player to represent his club at full international level for England. He was a big, bustling and powerfully built centre-forward, and was an awkward challenge for the Scottish defence. However, at this level, more was expected of you than just strength and aerial ability. Fashanu had been slammed in the press after a relatively dour performance in his debut against Chile. He'd not been the only one, but coming from an unfashionable club, he was an easy target. He'd partnered the elegant, yet unproven, Nigel Clough at Wembley, while on this occasion he had Everton's nippy striker Tony Cottee for company. Fashanu did show some promise when seven minutes into the proceedings he turned big defender Dave McPherson about halfway inside the Scottish half and burst towards the penalty area. However, he delayed his shot too long and was tackled by Stewart McKimmie.

The fast and furious pace didn't allow for opportunities in front of either goal early on, although Trevor Steven corner just over 12 minutes into the game almost brought the opening goal.

The Everton man, who Rangers manager Graeme Souness was rumoured to be interested in, saw his first kick headed over by Alex McLeish, though on the second attempt Steven found the head of Fashanu on the near post, whose faint touch almost saw England captain Bryan Robson scramble the ball in at the back post. It took a mighty scramble from McKimmie and Scotland skipper Roy Aitken to prevent Robson from knocking the ball home, and it would ultimately drift beyond them all and out for a goal kick. This was where Fashanu could prove very useful, though.

England were shading the opening 15 minutes. They seemed to have a slightly stronger grip in midfield, where Robson and Neil Webb appeared to be up for the battle. Scotland's pair, and also Celtic's engine room, Paul McStay and Roy Aitken, were both vastly experienced, and both battled hard to deny their opponents time and space. McStay seemed to be going head-to-head with Robson, while Aitken was enjoying a relatively free role, which allowed him to push forward on a couple of occasions.

McKimmie had spotted him to the right inside the English area on 11 minutes, and the defender's low ball into Aitken's feet almost brought about an opportunity for the home side, until Butcher nipped in to eventually play the ball back to Peter Shilton.

Six Scotland players had featured in the same fixture the year before, when England won 1-0 at Wembley. There were five for England. Peter Beardsley, absent this time on club duties, had scored the winner then.

Neither side was reluctant to use the long ball. Butcher looked for movement among the front two, and attempted to hit it into space for either of them to run on to. Balls were aimed at Fashanu's head, which the smaller Cottee tried to get on the end of. It had not been particularly fruitful in the first half, though a flick from Fashanu almost saw Webb get to the ball in the Scottish penalty area. Had Jim Leighton not been alert enough, some hesitancy among McKimmie and McLeish could've proved costly for Scotland. Webb, like Robson, was often so good at timing his runs from deep into the box.

This particular skill was something which the Scottish midfield duo could not match, at least not in this game. Webb and Robson would combine to set the captain up with an effort from inside the area, although the ball arrived to him a little awkwardly, and he could not get much power behind his attempt, which his Manchester United team-mate Leighton pushed away for another corner.

The opening goal of the game came on 20 minutes, and from perhaps one of the most unlikely of sources: Chris Waddle's head. England had built down the right, and it was a combination of the former Everton mates Gary Stevens and Trevor Steven which ultimately saw the full-back hit a first-time cross into the area. It eluded McLeish and found its way to just around the centre of the six-yard box, where Waddle sped towards the ball and met it with a bullet header which he planted high into the net just under the angle of the post and the bar. It was a fine assist and an even better header. Surely Waddle could not have scored a whole lot of headers throughout his career? The England fans in the open terrace behind Leighton's goal celebrated, and with the deadlock broken, it was time for Scotland to show what they were made of. They would need to produce a response.

The game continued in much the same vein after the goal, and Scotland at times looked a little lethargic, not showing enough quality to test the visiting back line. Quite conspicuous by its absence was Scottish wing play. They were operating with two midfield wide men in Pat Nevin along the right and Robert Connor to the left. The latter was appearing only for the third time in a Scotland jersey, and he seemed to struggle in finding his feet, perhaps being troubled by nerves. Connor would rather go inside or look for a pass backwards than take on Stevens, but, in truth, he was also not often in possession. Nevin down the other wing was not much more threatening, but at least he had shown a couple of glimpses of his ability, even if he was up against as tough an opponent for any winger as the hard left-back Stuart Pearce.

Behind Connor and Nevin were Maurice Malpas and Stewart McKimmie respectively, and while the two originally more forward players among the quartet had been silent so far, both McKimmie and Malpas had ventured across the halfway line. McKimmie had earlier found Aitken with the clever pass, and he'd shown defensive awareness in tackling Fashanu before the striker had been able to get a shot away. Malpas was providing typical solidity and was dependable both defensively and coming forward. Still, there had been little link-up with Connor, which also hampered Scotland down the left.

As for their opponents, goalscorer Waddle had been the most skilful performer on the pitch. Not rigidly tied down to the left-wing position, he looked to wander and use more or less the entire width of the pitch as he probed the Scotland defence. Even before his goal, he had troubled both full-backs with his trickery, and he would provide crosses from the left that the Scotland defence would need to be very alert to. Waddle had Pearce behind him, and while the Nottingham Forest defender was so often an attacking threat from the back, he had so far been happy to stay in his own half, allowing Waddle to shine.

The Stevens and Steven combination along the right was a tried and trusted weapon for England, as much as it had been for the great Everton side of the mid-to-late 1980s. Stevens had proved his crossing ability in assisting for the goal, while Steven actually had played more inside his own half rather than proving a threat to Malpas. He had got stuck in with a couple of challenges, but he was expected to provide balls into the centre from the right. England would have to give him more possession to do so and, earlier in the half, plenty had revolved around Waddle. In truth, Steven looked half fit.

On 22 minutes Peter Shilton spread himself well to deny McCoist as Scotland forced a corner. McCoist was finding it hard to make his mark as Butcher was always snapping at his heels. Mo Johnston began to drift wide against the pacy Walker as Scotland began to push England back.

In the game against Chile a few days earlier, Fashanu had needed to come off, with a knock to his left knee. When he took a kick from McStay in an innocuous-looking scrap for the ball well inside the Scottish half on 24 minutes, the big man needed medical attention, and it would turn out that the kick had struck in the very same place which had caused him to come off against the Latin Americans. While Fashanu would continue after some treatment, it was clear that he was no longer as mobile, and this would coincide with Scotland's best spell of the half as they were finally able to put England under a sustained period of pressure. Could Scotland take advantage, as without Fashanu, England would lack a physical presence up front?

The hosts put in some big challenges in midfield, where Aitken was showing his worth in battle, and there was almost an equaliser when the Scotland captain hit a ball into the centre of the English penalty area looking for McPherson, who had stayed up after a set-piece situation. England looked to have it under control and Shilton appeared to have told Walker that he was coming for the ball. At the last second, though, Walker decided that there had been enough hesitancy, and he booted it away for a corner just before Shilton, or McPherson, could reach it, a hairy moment.

The hapless Fashanu had to come off because of that earlier knock and on 32 minutes he was replaced by another fledgling at international level, Steve Bull. The man who had netted around 50 goals for club and country at under-21 and B levels since the start of the season came on for his debut, and he would become only the fifth player from the English Third Division to be given a full England cap.

Bull had been picked ahead of Nigel Clough, who was the other forward option on the substitutes' bench. However, the Nottingham Forest man had got his chance against the Chileans, and he had not really taken it. England manager Bobby Robson had said before the game that he would not be afraid to let Bull enter the fray. He remained true to his word.

With England now back with two strikers, albeit with a third-tier debutant now in their ranks, they seemed to raise their game again. Central midfield pair Webb and Robson were giving a solid account of themselves in the direct battle with Aitken and McStay. In fact, these duels would be key to getting the upper hand. Webb might not have been typically renowned for his battling skills, but he was no soft touch and, if anything, he was the most steady player for England in the centre of the pitch.

As for Bull's first few minutes on the turf, he looked a bit nervous, something which was understandable, even if he had recently returned from a tour with the England B team, in which he'd scored twice in three matches, against Switzerland, Iceland and Norway. His very first battle in full England colours was against Maurice Malpas, and the home defender came out on top, although it was clear that Bull had displayed a great mentality in always wanting to give chase, and not letting the home defenders have even a few seconds' peace.

His striker partner Cottee also did this, but seemingly to less effect. Cottee didn't have Bull's physical attributes, and he had largely been anonymous to that point, finding it difficult to get going against a strong central defensive pairing of McLeish and McPherson.

For Scotland, it would have been unfair to label them 'long ball merchants', but, of the two teams, they were the more direct. As had already been seen so far in the World Cup qualification campaign, Johnston and his partner McCoist could both get on the end of such balls, although the service they were receiving in this match had not been angled out into the channels to find them.

This reduced the hosts' ability to stretch the visiting defence, ensuring that England had lived a relatively worry-free existence during the first half. There had been a possible opening for Scotland on 35 minutes from Malpas's opportunistic header into the centre of the area, but although Johnston had momentarily managed to free himself of any attention, he had been unable to control the ball, which would end up in safe Shilton's hands.

The first half continued through to a 47th minute with most of the additional time for the treatment of Fashanu. It would be an overstatement to say that the game opened up towards the end of the half, although there would be a couple of opportunities coming in both directions, even if creative play was not always easy to spot. Scotland's two half-chances came from long-distance efforts through Aitken and McStay, who were both given the opportunity to shoot from more than 20 yards. Aitken's drive was set up by Nevin, who had come across to the left to feed his captain an angled ball backwards, though Shilton always saw the effort drift wide to the left. Just before the half-time whistle, McStay had an opportunity after England had failed to properly clear the ball following an attacking set piece from the hosts. McStay had struck the ball on the volley from 22 yards, but he failed to get much conviction behind his effort, which bounced once off the grass before it ended up in the grasp of Shilton.

It had been a decent spectacle, with not a lot of stoppages. England could go into their dressing room relatively pleased with both scoreline and their performance, holding a deserved lead, while the hosts would need to find more creativity inside the final third of the pitch. With Nevin seeing more of the ball in the final few minutes, perhaps his involvement could prove fruitful after the break?

The crowd had been treated to marching bands of bagpipe musicians during the break; then as the second half kicked off both managers kept faith in their respective sets of players and no substitutions were made. Incidentally, that Waddle goal was England's 187th overall in meetings with Scotland. The hosts had amassed 168 until now.

The first few minutes of the second half were pulsating. Neither team appeared to have any wish to just sit back and invite the other on to them, and they both managed to have a go in the first few minutes of a frantic opening. Aberdeen full-back McKimmie was the first to test Shilton when he accepted a short free kick from McStay inside the English half, before he went on to fire a left-footed effort from 25 yards which was comfortably held by the stopper.

Just shy of two minutes in, Nevin was close to breaking through inside the English area after a one-two with Johnston, who cleverly attempted to lay the ball back into the nippy winger's path, though it was ultimately played too close to Shilton, who again gathered the ball.

While Scotland had had a couple of attempts, the visitors then had three efforts of their own. First up was the inspired Bull, who took down a 50-yard pass from Waddle in the right-sided channel. He set his sights on goal and fired a rocket just to the left of the upright from the far side of the area.

A couple of minutes later, Steven tried something similar but he saw the ball drift the wrong side of the post. In between those two shots, Waddle had tried to chip Leighton from inside the area after a neat one-two with Cottee, but under pressure from the recovering McKimmie the skilful winger put too much weight under the ball, and the chip cleared the bar by a yard.

There were yellow cards for McLeish and Robson but overall the French referee Michel Vautrot was letting the game flow. Bull, to his credit, didn't make a meal of being on the receiving end from McLeish, even if it must have been a painful challenge, and he dusted himself off and got on with the game. Bull had started the second half with a fire in his belly, and McLeish's tackle could well have been an attempt to leave a marker. If anything, it just seemed to enrage the striker.

There had been a tasty opening to the second half. It was not as if the first 45 minutes had been dreary, but now there were opportunities in either direction, even if the hosts' chances of scoring had not yet been quite as clear-cut as those of the visiting English. If the game continued in the same vein, it seemed impossible that it would finish with just Waddle's name on the score sheet.

It was pretty much end-to-end by now, although you continually had the feeling that England had more quality about them, whereas Scotland were left to a greater extent looking for a moment of opportunism from their players. At the back for the visitors, Walker and Butcher appeared to complement each other, with the former's pace and the latter's brute strength. It also appeared that while Butcher had been narking Johnston in the early first-half proceedings, he had more or less switched his attention towards his Ibrox compatriot McCoist since. The home team's number nine did not appear to be at his sharpest, and so this was a contest that, so far, was winning quite comfortably, even if you could never count a goalscorer of McCoist's stature completely out.

In midfield, Webb and Robson were dominating Aitken and McStay. While Robson was always a powerful opponent, Webb was probably outshining him with some tough tackling of his own, and in addition to physicality, he could also draw on a high level of football intelligence. He would in general be the more advanced of the pair, and he would support the strikers inside the final third of the pitch. Webb already had a chipped effort early in the second half from outside the area that drifted harmlessly wide.

With Scottish wing play at a minimum, they would need to carve out openings through the centre, not a simple task against such a strong English defence. However, a fine chance went Johnston's way on 54 minutes, as he was allowed to take a McStay pass down on his chest inside the area, with right-back Stevens not sticking to him tight enough. Johnston, the UEFA zone's leading World Cup qualification marksman with six goals from five matches, should have done better with his shot, as he failed to get much power behind it from 12 yards. Shilton comfortably collected the weak effort.

Less than a minute later, McCoist was able to swing his boot at the ball, although his low shot from the right inside the area was a feeble one that was no trouble for the experienced England goalkeeper. There was another attempt on goal when McStay found plenty of space inside the English half. He did not need a second invitation to run forward and he let fly, though his shot from 25 yards lacked the necessary power to trouble Shilton, who gathered comfortably.

When the change happened on 57 minutes it proved to be the very first introduction to full international football for Celtic's 23-year-old midfielder Peter Grant. Off came the poor Robert Connor, who had seemed completely inadequate as a left-sided midfielder. With two of his Parkhead compatriots already occupying central midfield berths, however, would Grant slot directly into the space left vacant by Connor along the left?

The substitution did appear to give the home side a lift. Grant slotted right into the centre of the pitch, with Aitken moving out towards the left. It was clear to everyone who knew about Roy Aitken's ability as a footballer that as good as he was, he was clearly no winger. However, what you would get from him was someone who gave 100 per cent whatever position he was played in. Although he would not attempt to take Steven and/or Stevens on, he would swing in a couple of crosses from deep positions. Grant, on the other hand, looked fearless in the few minutes since his introduction. He won an aerial challenge against Robson and he appeared confident and prepared to win the midfield battle for the hosts. However, with Webb alongside him, the Manchester United captain looked imperious and the pair were dominant.

Scotland created their biggest opportunity, yet on the hour, when McKimmie threaded a pass through into space for McCoist to run on to, and this time the striker managed to get to the ball ahead of Butcher. McCoist was in behind the English defence, but Shilton did a great job in racing off his line to give him no time, which made him hurry his shot, which the keeper got his hands to. The ball cannoned back off McCoist and would sneak just wide of Shilton's upright. It had been agonisingly close for the hosts. A long-distance effort by Grant was saved by Shilton down to his right a few minutes later; the England defence stood firm under pressure, but Scotland were certainly asking the questions.

Wing play was sadly absent for both teams. England definitely seemed to be equipped with more quality in those positions, but they failed to make use of them, or perhaps they were reluctant to do so after Bobby Robson's instructions. Why would they not try to make more out of Waddle, who had been lively for spells during the first half?

The combination of Gary Stevens and Trevor Steven on the right had been really disappointing, with Steven not on his best form. Stevens had provided the cross for the goal, and closed down his side defensively. Steven had taken a knock midway through the second half, something which could've kept him quiet for the latter stages, but had been largely ineffectual up until that point anyway.

Scotland could've proved a bigger threat had their two wingers been prepared to take on the England defence. A few minutes after their substitution, Andy Roxburgh decided to switch sides for Aitken and Nevin, with the latter moving towards the left in order to try and cause some problems to Stevens. Nevin was keen, but he wasn't being given the ball by his team-mates. With 73 minutes gone, he managed to dribble to the edge of the area from the left, only to see his eventual effort on goal blocked by the alert Walker.

One of the most disappointing aspects of the Scotland display had been the lack of service to Johnston, who had nothing to feed on, no through balls or crosses into the box. He could get no change out of Butcher and Walker. Nevin had a frustrating game, constantly drifting inside from the right, into the congested central midfield. So he provided no width. On the left, Robert Connor had seemed overawed and was a virtual spectator.

England were regaining their composure by the time that they made their second substitution. They had been in the ascendancy for the past couple of minutes, with the Scottish enthusiasm levels having taken a slight hit, at least for the time being. Perhaps the game was about to peter out comfortably in the end for the visitors, who had come under some pressure since the start of the second half. On came Paul Gascoigne for Cottee after 75 minutes.

In taking off Cottee, who had largely been anonymous, and bringing on Gascoigne, for the young Geordie's fifth cap, Bobby Robson would bolster his central midfield with an additional man. Long before the 4-2-3-1 formation would become well known, this was how England seemed to line up, with Webb and Robson sitting in holding roles behind Gascoigne, who would try and be the creative link behind the rampaging Bull.

Then out of nothing England increased their lead. The goal came courtesy of Bull, who did well once Gary Stevens knocked a ball towards the edge of the area. Bull managed to win an aerial challenge with the tall McPherson. It had not struck Bull's head, but rather the back of his shoulder, which ensured that the ball didn't travel far, and once he'd orientated himself, he would strike first time right-footed from just inside the area. The shot was firm, and it ended up in the bottom corner past Leighton, who had no chance. This was something of a fairy tale, with a player from the third tier notching a goal on his full international debut.

Scotland could no longer manage to pin England back, and so the game was over as a contest after the second goal. If anything, the visitors could've added further insult to injury when Bull accepted a long, booted clearance from his own half by Pearce. He easily advanced past the hesitant McPherson, and also rounded McKimmie, but having subsequently lost his balance, and with Leighton coming off his line to close him down, Bull could only hit his left-footed effort straight into the chest of the keeper.

And just another minute after that, Gascoigne showed his technical ability along the right, from where he cut into the area beyond McLeish, but in trying to be clever and finish with the outside of his right boot from an angle, the talented Tottenham Hotspur star saw Leighton parry his shot. The goalkeeper now stood between the hosts and an embarrassing scoreline.

As the crowd began to stream out of Hampden in the last five minutes, McStay fired over a free kick from the edge of the box, but Scotland could not force a consolation goal.

It was a sobering defeat. Andy Roxburgh had not seen Scotland score a goal in any of his three matches against England, following a 0-0 draw at Hampden in 1987 and a 1-0 defeat at Wembley in 1988. They had been overpowered in midfield as Aitken and McStay were no match for Bryan Robson and Neil Webb. Des Walker and Terry Butcher had dealt with any threat by Mo Johnston and Ally McCoist and, in truth, Scotland rarely looked like scoring. England had too much quality, Chris Waddle was in great form and they were able to bring on an outstanding player, Paul Gascoigne, in the second half. England won the Rous Cup for the third time and this was to be the last annual game between the two rivals.

30 May 1989 – Scotland 2 Chile 0

Just 9,000 fans turned up to see Jim Leighton win his 50th cap and captain the side. This ensured him free tickets for all future Scotland internationals. An early Alan McInally goal when he stabbed home from a corner, and a second-half MacLeod strike from long range – both men scoring their first goals for their country – ensured that Scotland finished second in the 1989 Rous Cup.

Leighton (c)
McKimmie–Gillespie (Whyte 70)–McLeish–Malpas
Grant–Aitken–McStay–MacLeod
Speedie (Johnston HT)–McInally

11

Collapse in Yugoslavia

6 September 1989 – Yugoslavia 3 Scotland 1

HERE WERE teams in an excellent position to qualify for Italia 90: a draw would have been enough for Scotland, while Yugoslavia needed a win, and one of them would have been able to secure a place at the 1990 World Cup at the end of this night.

Remarkably, Yugoslavia boss Ivica Osim named an XI with no designated right wing-back, in a lopsided 4-4-2. Vujadin Stanojković had been ever-present in qualification so far in the right wing-back position, but was relegated to the substitutes' bench this time as Osim evidently found that his position was surplus to requirements.

Compared to the 5-4-1 used in the previous qualifiers, Osim sacrificed Stanojković and added an extra striker. That additional forward was Dragan Jakovljević, who recently had switched to play in France for Nantes.

Osim revealed to the media that he had been unsure whether to play Jakovljević or Dejan Savićević. Once again, the latter needed to be content with a place among the substitutes, something he had publicly announced he was unhappy with, and which had caused some unrest after the game against Norway in June.

Regular libero Davor Jozić was suspended after being sent off against Norway in their last qualifier. In his absence, Osim drafted in Mirsad Baljić as a new stopper, with Faruk Hadžibegić moving to the vacant libero position. Baljić was usually a left wing-back by trade, but his position in this match would clearly be a man-marking stopper along with Predrag Spasić. At left wing-back, Osim had instead trusted Dragoljub Brnović, who had been a regular in the squad so far in qualification, but only once previously started a qualifier.

There was no surprise formation-wise from Andy Roxburgh: 4-4-2. In midfield, he had pondered whether to play Murdo MacLeod or Peter Grant on the left, the position in the team that had troubled him the most so far in the group. In any event, MacLeod or Grant would become the sixth different player thus to play in that position. Roxburgh eventually opted for MacLeod, who would play as a left-sided midfielder when Scotland were in possession, but would tuck inside to assist Aitken and McStay against Yugoslavia's attempts to penetrate through the middle.

Both MacLeod and Grant were by nature central midfielders, known for their battling skills, not wide players. The lack of options meant that Roxburgh simply had to play someone out of position as he had done with Ian Ferguson previously, but the Rangers man was ruled out with injury.

Mo Johnston was injured, meaning that Roxburgh only had McCoist available from his favoured striker duo. To partner him, Roxburgh had the choice of Gordon Durie and Alan McInally. The decision to play Durie gave the team more options when breaking forward, as the Scots looked to hit the hosts on the break.

In defence, Richard Gough had been a revelation so far in qualification, not the least thanks to his towering headers, which were proving a real goalscoring threat. Sadly, he was injured this time, meaning that the reliable Gary Gillespie would play at right-back, a task he had done well away in Norway, earlier in the group. Surprisingly, there was no sign of Stewart McKimmie, who had played twice for Scotland in the Rous Cup.

The full line-up was:

Leighton
Gillespie–Miller–McLeish–Malpas
Nicol–Aitken (c)–McStay–MacLeod
Durie (McInally 68)–McCoist

There were two different styles clashing in Zagreb: Osim's Yugoslavia in a fluid 4-4-2 shape versus Roxburgh's more rigid 4-4-2.

Roxburgh had, however, made one alteration to the traditional 4-4-2 formula, instructing Murdo MacLeod to tuck inside to assist Aitken and McStay when Scotland were not in possession of the ball. Roxburgh must have been well aware of Yugoslavia's ability to dominate possession in the central area, as witnessed in their latest qualifiers, and had deemed that an extra man would be useful in stopping the attacking movements of Stojković et al.

This seemed like a good ploy, but it was a measure that proved to have only limited effect. Yugoslavia's midfield quartet dominated play just as much as they had done in the previous qualifiers, as they frequently penetrated the Scottish midfield and played through balls to the forwards.

For large parts of the half, Scotland were outpassed and outplayed.

While Scotland's central midfield might have had an additional man in MacLeod, their pressing and positioning was poor overall. MacLeod, McStay and Aitken were at times completely disjointed, and the Yugoslavian midfielders were usually able to simply play around them. Scotland's pressing would have needed to be much better organised, and McCoist and Durie more focussed on Baždarević and Srečko Katanec rather than closing down defenders.

Roy Aitken in particular had a night to forget. He constantly looked too slow and did an ineffectual job in closing down opponents. Space between the Scottish defence and midfield was compact, though, and McLeish and Miller did their best to intercept whenever Yugoslavia were penetrating a weak and disjointed midfield department. At one point, it seemed that Yugoslavia were able to work the ball into dangerous areas every time they went forward.

Yugoslavia's domination was once again built around the strong, fluid midfield quartet that they had become used to: Sušić, Stojković, Baždarević and Katanec. So far in the group they had used Stojković as a right-sided midfielder with much freedom, frequently drifting inside to command play in the central area. Here, however, he had a free role in the centre of the field, and rarely moved into wide positions on either side at all.

Katanec was again, as against Norway last time, reluctant to join attacks. Previously in qualification he had frequently shuttled forward and acted almost as a second striker at times, using his aerial abilities and goalscoring abilities in the penalty area. But with Jakovljević in the side and the need to keep an eye on any Scottish moves down the right, Osim had likely told Katanec to be more cautious.

Baždarević and Sušić had roles similar to what they had in the last qualifiers. Notably, with Stojković in a more central position, there was less need for Baždarević to orchestrate play, and hence there was less seen of his sweeping passes. Sušić was again sitting on top of Yugoslavia's midfield, in the narrow gap between Scotland's defence and midfield, and looked to play through balls for the two forwards whenever he received possession.

With Osim's formation not including a designated right wing-back, there was someone on the opposite side, Dragoljub Brnović. Moreover, as MacLeod tucked inside, unusually large areas of space could be seen opening up on the home side's right flank whenever Yugoslavia were in possession of the ball.

The three central defenders, Spasić, Baljić and Hadžibegić, took turns to motor into this space whenever they saw fit. This could have proved useful to Scotland if Yugoslavia's attacking movement had been halted, as they always had a release option down the right. The defender shuttling forward was usually able to advance high up the field without any Scottish player closing him down, and this provided Yugoslavia with some very good opportunities for crosses.

Seemingly alert to Yugoslavia's intent to penetrate through the middle, Scotland defended narrowly. In particular, Gillespie, at right-back, kept a tight distance between himself and Willie Miller. Roxburgh had clearly felt that his side could sacrifice some space in the wide areas in order to consolidate in the middle. They would then stand a better chance clearing crosses.

It was a pattern in Yugoslavia's qualifiers that they rarely threatened down the flanks except through the wing-backs, which meant that they rarely created two-on-one situations. The idea was for the wing-back to motor forward and work the ball into the box, and nobody performed this task better in the first half in Zagreb than Dragoljub Brnović. Brnović was a better option for Yugoslavia in games where they really attacked their opponents, while Zoran Vujović seemed to be the better option when Osim wanted more defensive balance.

Gillespie's tendency to tuck inside meant that there were large areas to be exploited for Brnović, and Steve Nicol made surprisingly little effort to track him down. Stojković regularly managed to thread the ball between Nicol and Gillespie, to release Brnović who was darting forward and putting in a large number of crosses, usually of good quality. Roxburgh was, however, right to assume that his defenders would mostly manage to deal with these situations and not even the tall Jakovljević managed to get on the end of them. Perhaps Brnović should have considered a low cut-back now and then instead of just whipping the ball in. Yugoslavia were dominating possession but that was to be expected with them knowing a victory would send them to the finals.

Scotland's approach was cautious, and they didn't offer a lot going forward. One of their best attacking weapons was whenever McCoist came short to lay the ball off to a team-mate who was moving forward. The Rangers striker worked unselfishly and was able to spot spaces for his colleagues to run into. Durie was less involved than McCoist, but generally did look sharp. His movement was good, but there was just too little support from midfield. McCoist did well to make transitions between midfield and attack, but Scotland were reluctant to commit men forward and most of their movements soon came to a halt at the edge of the Yugoslav penalty area.

The Scots were trying to keep possession and stroke the ball around, trying to slow the tempo of the game. However, there were too many sloppy passes that simply handed possession over to the hosts. Paul McStay needed to get hold of the ball and use his quality to create.

Despite Yugoslavia's domination, it was Scotland who took the lead in the 43rd minute, after being awarded a free kick and having moved players forward. Instead of hoisting the ball into the box, MacLeod and McStay played a short free kick that set up McCoist against Spasić on the edge of the penalty area. The tireless McCoist made a quick turn to escape his marker and crossed towards the far post, above backtracking defenders who misjudged the flight of the ball, and it fell perfectly for Durie to steer a powerful header into the net.

In fact, this was quite possibly Scotland's second good goal of the game, as McCoist had scored earlier on but it had been disallowed on dubious grounds. It also followed from a free kick pumped into the box, where McCoist had latched on to a knock-down from Gary Gillespie. The referee quickly ruled it out, but why? Offside? Free kick against Gillespie? Television replays provided no conclusive answer.

It was a big concern for Osim that Yugoslavia had been unable to capitalise on their dominance, and were a goal down at the interval. Scotland were now just 45 minutes away from reaching their fifth World Cup in a row.

Yugoslavia came right out after the break and were piling on the pressure with the same pattern as the first half, before scoring three goals in quick succession. The equaliser came on 54 minutes. Baljić had found space to receive the ball down the right flank, as he exploited the notorious gap in the visitors' defence. MacLeod quickly spotted his run and tried to close him down but slipped and fell over, which gave Baljić plenty of time to deliver the ball into the box. Towering above Jim Leighton – as well as Vujović and Jakovljević – was Katanec, who arrived late in the area to crash in a powerful header. Katanec had been reluctant to join attacks in just the last couple of games, but here fully demonstrated what a very capable player he was for Yugoslavia at crosses. Leighton and Scotland's central defenders were well beaten in the air and Aitken, who had noticed Katanec, did nothing to track his run.

Yugoslavia went 2-1 up on 58 minutes after an own goal by Steve Nicol, in an ill-fated attempt to clear a free kick swung in by Stojković. Under pressure from a flighted ball to the back post, he headed it past Leighton.

Things got even worse for Scotland just one minute later, and at this point they were in disarray. First, Sušić evaded a couple of tackles in midfield before spotting Vujović on an angling run. His perfect pass set up Vujović one-on-one with Gillespie. Vujović's attempted cross took a wicked deflection off Gillespie, which entirely deceived Leighton, and with the keeper out of position the ball flew past him.

Scotland had been ripped to shreds within the space of six minutes, so their understandable priority after the third goal was damage control. Three goals in less than six minutes killed any belief they might have had of getting a result from this match. There were no signs of any immediate attempt to stage a comeback, as Scotland focussed on saving what was left. Yugoslavia, on their part, were understandably happy with the score and not too interested in attacking. The rest of the game was therefore largely an uneventful affair, only mixed with a few ill-tempered moments.

Roxburgh made one change to his personnel, as he brought on Alan McInally for Gordon Durie. In the 74th minute Osim introduced Savićević for Jakovljević. The swap did look an improvement, as the fresh legs of Savićević were able to find spaces in the tiring Scotland side. He looked determined to prove his worth, and probably had more involvement than Jakovljević had managed the entire game, although he also failed to deliver a lot of end product and seemed frustrated at his lack of impact. Scotland huffed and puffed but could not get back into the game and in the end it was a comfortable 3-1 win for Yugoslavia.

At full time Roxburgh seemed shell-shocked. From being ahead at the interval and looking quite solid, his team had collapsed in the second half, losing three bad goals. Once again, Leighton was at fault, coming for and missing a cross for the equaliser. The own goals by Nicol and Gillespie were unfortunate, but Leighton looked badly out of position for the third goal.

The talented Yugoslavs were worthy winners and in captain Dragan Stojković they had a world-class playmaker. The defeat underlined that the 34-year-old defender Willie Miller looked like his best days were behind him. His partner at Aberdeen, Alex McLeish, was still only 30. He looked more solid alongside Dave McPherson or Gary Gillespie. The pace of Hearts defender Craig Levein might have also been an option to tighten things up. Stewart McKimmie could consider himself unlucky not to start at right-back.

Up front, Scotland badly missed the movement and finishing power of Mo Johnston. He could have been ideally suited to break down a packed defence, just as he had done scoring twice against France at Hampden. Gordon Durie had shown some promising touches and Ally McCoist looked sharp, and capable of making something out of nothing.

The defeat underlined the limitations of Roy Aitken and Paul McStay as a central midfield pair at international level, as neither had the legs or the energy to close down or push back their more technically gifted opponents. Neither looked like scoring either. Steve Nicol and Murdo MacLeod were both honest and hard-working players, but neither were natural right- or left-wingers. MacLeod was 30 and at times it showed. Nicol was 27 and still had plenty of drive and energy. His own goal was a result of panic at the heart of the Scottish defence. McLeish or Miller should have been picking up the Yugoslavia runners, but the Liverpool man got there first to head past Leighton.

Would Roxburgh revert back to a back three and a 3-5-2 formation in Paris the following month? Scotland had seemed secure in their previous qualifiers but now defending well was vital. They needed just a point in Paris or at Hampden against Norway.

With more creativity needed, would Roxburgh opt for Pat Nevin or the in-form Gordon Strachan, who was enjoying a great season at Leeds United? Could Motherwell's Davie Cooper earn a shock call-up? With Johnston to come back and the options of McInally and Durie off the bench, Scotland still looked like they had a goal threat. It was keeping clean sheets that was the problem.

France knew it was win or bust in Paris in October 1989, and Michel Platini's men would be formidable opponents at the Parc des Princes. With top-class players like Franck Sauzée, Didier Deschamps and the exciting forward Eric

Cantona, few people gave Scotland much of a chance of getting a result but Roxburgh still believed in his men, and knew that they always seemed to perform better when they were underdogs. With a vocal Scottish support, there was no reason why they couldn't get something against the French.

12

French Flair

11 October 1989 – France 3 Scotland 0

THE GAME kicked off with both teams aware of the fact that anything other than a home win would send Scotland through to the World Cup. There had perhaps been a vague hope, certainly more in France than in Scotland, that Norway would go on and win in Yugoslavia, but that match had kicked off more than two hours earlier, and news of the 1-0 success for the Yugoslavs would gradually make its way around the French national stadium with kick-off looming. A victory for the visitors would've taken the Scandinavians up to seven points, with qualification still to play for when they visited Glasgow in the final round of matches. Now, all France could do was win this one, and then hope for a late miracle in the middle of the following month.

Yugoslavia's passage through to Italia 90 had already been guaranteed even before that win against Norway, and now it would almost be impossible to deny them top spot in the group. Their remaining game was away, albeit played on neutral ground, to Cyprus.

France manager Michel Platini had picked a squad of 16 without two notable absentees: full-back and team captain Manuel Amoros and star striker Jean-Pierre Papin. They were the only two players absent since their previous qualifier, the 1-1 draw in Norway the previous month.

Drafted into *Les Bleus*' squad as replacements for the two absent players were left-footed centre-half Bernard Casoni of Toulon and creative forward Daniel Bravo of Paris Saint-Germain. Casoni, 28, had played the full 90 minutes in both of France's first two qualifiers, and was then an unused substitute during the 2-0 loss in Scotland, while 26-year-old Bravo had also played in those two first qualification matches, before coming on as a substitute in the 3-2 loss in Yugoslavia late in 1988.

It was a well-balanced squad that was available to Platini and coach Gérard Houllier. The starting 11 would not differ much from their last outing, while Scotland went for:

Leighton

Nicol–Gough–McLeish–Malpas

Strachan (McInally 74)–Aitken (c)–McStay–MacLeod (Bett 76)

Johnston–McCoist

The Scots were also without Dundee United's young forward Kevin Gallacher, who had just made a solitary qualification appearance to date. He had been an unused substitute on four occasions.

In the squad that travelled to Paris, 11 of the players from Yugoslavia remained. This meant five had been omitted for various reasons since the previous month: Gary Gillespie, Willie Miller, Steve Clarke, Peter Grant and Gordon Durie. Coming into the squad for the quintet were defenders

Richard Gough and Dave McPherson, midfielders Gordon Strachan and Jim Bett, as well as striker Mo Johnston. The latter had scored six times in six qualifiers, and his return was a very welcome one. With Durie out this time, Johnston, whose command of the French language was quite sound after his time at Nantes, looked set to partner Rangers teammate Ally McCoist up top. The latter had started each of Scotland's four most recent qualifiers.

It was an experienced squad, although there did not appear to be a whole lot of pace in there. The Scots would probably need to exploit chances on the counter attack to return home from the French capital with that point which would ensure their qualification.

The Parc des Princes had staged France internationals for 84 years already, and this was the 117th to take place there. Not since a 1975 qualifier for the following year's European Championship had France played a home qualifier outside of their metropolis: They had beaten Iceland 3-0 in Nantes back then.

Despite Scotland's setback in Yugoslavia, they were not in France just to sit back and soak up the pressure. They started the game in a very collected manner, determined not to give anything away early on. However, they were up against the equally committed hosts who put in some hefty early challenges as they showed that they did not wish to relinquish any initiative.

There were early free kicks against Bernard Pardo, Didier Deschamps and Yvon Le Roux for fouls, of which the latter was a big tackle from behind on McCoist. The striker required physio treatment before play could resume.

The game started at a slow pace and the visitors almost struck first on nine minutes through McCoist, who attempted a half-volley from the left edge of the 18-yard area. His looped effort flew just wide of the post with Joël Bats beaten. Five minutes later, Pardo's hopeful volley from 25 yards sailed well over.

Scotland were keeping their shape well and France were left with little room in which to mount attacks. The Scots looked better than they had done in Zagreb, but they were also not facing an opponent with players of such individual talent. This French midfield did not boast talent akin to that of Dragan Stojković, but they compensated for that with plenty of battling skills and strong running. It was Scotland, however, who had the first effort on target 17 minutes in, when big centre-back Gough rose well deep in the penalty area following Strachan's raking corner from the right wing.

Gough connected cleanly despite the presence of Franck Sauzée, and his firm, downward header forced a vital save from Bats low down. The keeper clutched the rebound with Johnston ready to pounce to put the ball in the net.

The opening 25 minutes of the game were a stalemate as the hosts struggled to wriggle free from the tight Scottish marking. Another right-wing corner routine from Strachan on 24 minutes found the towering Gough in an identical spot and once again Sauzée was no match in the air for the defender, Gough making Bats work from his downward header. It bounced up just in front of the keeper, who collected the ball safely at the second time of asking to deny McCoist and Johnston any chance of a rebound.

While France had created little so far, they struck first when they capitalised on some sloppy Scottish play inside their own half. Firstly, it was Gough who failed to find left-back Malpas with a simple ball from the centre, and from Eric Cantona's throw-in along the right, the French managed to create an attack that involved several players, Christian Perez, Pardo, Deschamps, Jean-Marc Ferreri and, ultimately, Perez again. The little PSG forward picked Deschamps out with a deft pass from the outside of his right foot. Deschamps seized on the chance and he placed a low shot to the left of Leighton, just inside the near post and into the back of the net.

With Amoros and Papin out, for this fixture Platini had to tinker somewhat with his tactics. Admittedly, the 4-3-3 had not looked a great fit until the sudden goal, as they had struggled to get going, rarely creating enough movement off the ball to provide team-mates with passing options. The French had looked sound in 4-4-2 in their two matches away against Nordic opposition, but the absence of goal poacher Papin had made them return to 4-3-3, the formation they'd used in the home game against Yugoslavia back in April.

In Amoros's absence, 32-year-old Paris Saint-Germain goalkeeper Bats was given the captain's armband. It was his 49th appearance for France, and though his error had gifted Norway a late equaliser during that 1-1 draw in Oslo in September, the management team clearly had few qualms about selecting him once again.

In the centre, Sauzée and the experienced Le Roux, who perhaps was best remembered for his sending-off during the final of the 1984 European Championship, on home soil, where he had to see the final few minutes of the 2-0 win against Spain from the touchline, were paired for a third successive international. Le Roux had somewhat struggled lately with injuries, and had also come off in the second half the previous month, but his availability was a boost for Platini. Sauzée was once again France's libero, and with the Marseille man being such a good reader of the game, he seemed ideal at instigating from the back.

The three-man-strong midfield consisted of Bordeaux team-mates Bernard Pardo and Jean-Philippe Durand, as well as Nantes captain Didier Deschamps, a 20-year-old player with such tenacity and skill. Durand had a role on the right, while Pardo was a defensive midfielder. Pardo was a decent player in possession and would often look for team-mates further up the pitch.

He had the ability to thread a ball through the opposition's midfield. Durand and Deschamps worked well defensively: there was perhaps not a great deal of flair among them, but against Scotland they would first and foremost need to win the battle. Then they could look to play.

With no Papin available, Eric Cantona had been given the lone task through the centre, although it should be said that his role was quite similar to what we'd seen from Papin earlier. Cantona would play as deep-lying forward and though there was no talk yet of a 'false nine', this was probably what his position was in reality. With the midfield three looking to utilise their battling ability rather than create, Cantona would time and again drop deep to take part in the build-up. He certainly had an eye for the spectacular even at this early stage in his career, and the 23-year-old Montpellier forward was a constant threat.

Jean-Marc Ferreri, the third Bordeaux starter in the starting 11, had switched from his position wide on the right of midfield in a 4-4-2 to the left-sided forward now in a 4-3-3. He was winning his 30th cap, and while he'd been guilty for failing to tuck a second French goal away just before the break in their last qualifier, he seemed more or less a foregone conclusion for Platini to select him. He rarely accelerated at blistering speed, but he kept excellent control of the ball, and also knew when to pick the right moment for a pass. He was often a set-piece taker, particularly for corners, and was altogether a very useful inclusion.

Perhaps less predictable was right-sided forward Christian Perez, the 26-year-old of PSG, who featured for the sixth time. Perez had been France's left-sided midfielder in their most recent 4-4-2 line-ups, but he seemed to relish linking up with Franck Silvestre, Durand and sometimes also Cantona towards the right. He would often cut inside, and he had played a vital role in the build-up to the goal. He was quick and nimble, and someone who opponents would often struggle to mark.

One of the trademarks of a good side is their ability to bounce back after going a goal down. So how about this Scotland side: did they have it in them? They had been having the greater share of possession prior to going behind, and they had seemed far from being overawed by the occasion. Their many supporters who had travelled were still in fine voice, and that had helped give the team a lift from the start. Still, they were now a goal down, and though a second straight qualifying loss would be disappointing, they would still have another opportunity in their final qualifier the following month. That said, they did not want to surrender in Paris without a fight.

Andy Roxburgh had, naturally, lined his charges up in 4-4-2 again, for a seventh time in qualification. Clearly, he had been far from impressed during their 2-0 loss in Italy the previous December, their solitary game in this period where they'd deviated from four at the back. What seemed to be lacking, though, was pace. Scotland were sluggish at the back, did not boast plenty of pace or power through midfield or down the flanks, and even up top there was not much speed, even if Johnston was the quickest of the strikers.

At right-back, Liverpool stalwart Steve Nicol, 27, also started for the sixth time in qualifying, although for the first time as a full-back. He had started wide in midfield on each of his previous appearances. Also, he would not be seen on a lot of marauding runs from his position and, as such, he was clearly less useful than Richard Gough, who had featured several times in this role since the start of the campaign. Gough had on this occasion, though, been thrust into the centre, with no Willie Miller available to partner Alex McLeish.

It was Gough's first outing at centre-back in qualification. He had arrived for attacking headers following a series of right-wing corners from Strachan, and so far had rarely been challenged defensively. However, his sloppiness in failing to find Malpas with a simple pass saw Scotland concede the throw from which France would ultimately score to move in front.

While Gough looked after right-central areas, McLeish, as usual, was Scotland's left-sided centre-half. Gough was sitting somewhat deeper, almost in the sweeper-like role in which Miller had previously performed, with McLeish typically giving his all in challenges both along the ground and in the air. So far, McLeish, the 30-year-old Aberdeen man making his 65th appearance for his country, the highest in this starting 11, had often come in contact with either Perez or Durand. The relatively deep-lying Cantona had eluded him thus far.

To his left, McLeish had the ever-reliable Maurice Malpas. The Dundee United left-back, 27, was making his 30th Scotland appearance. He was one of three ever-presents for the Scots in the current qualification, and was a steady customer along the left, where he would use either foot to find a team-mate. Malpas was less attacking than in most of Scotland's previous qualifiers.

In the centre of midfield, Scotland had Celtic pair Roy Aitken, team captain and 30 years of age, and Paul McStay, 24 and winning his 40th cap, for a seventh successive qualifier. While McStay had often directed their midfield play, and had certainly done so more successfully early in qualification rather than of late, Aitken had at times looked somewhat below par, not always keeping up with their opponents. While McStay had quick feet, Aitken struggled to keep pace, and was it perhaps a fair question to ask whether he was still an asset to the team. As a leader: certainly. However, in open play? He would display his usual commitment, but France's midfield would eventually find a way around him, while McStay's playmaking ability would be less evident as the game went on. Perhaps he suffered from having generally slow players around him. McStay appeared to thrive when he could look to pin a pass into space for either forward to run on to, or when making a trademark bursting run through the centre.

For the wide positions, Scotland had recalled Gordon Strachan on the right. Aged 32 and now playing in the second tier in England with Leeds, the flame-haired action man was not without experience, but he lacked pace, and he would rather cut inside than try to take his full-back on to get into a crossing position. While this could've paved the way for Nicol to attack from the right-back position, it made Scotland a little too narrow.

Instead, it would be Johnston who would look to utilise wide-right areas or the right-sided channels. Opposite from Strachan was 31-year-old Murdo MacLeod, yet another player far from quick enough to make it past his full-back. The West Germany-based wide man was playing for his country for the 11th time, and while he possessed an excellent left foot, his crosses would always come from deep positions, and were easier to defend than those coming from higher up the pitch.

Usually thriving from attacking wing play was striker Ally McCoist, who had turned 27 since their last outing, and whose return of one goal in the ongoing campaign had probably been a bit disappointing considering his reputation on the domestic scene. A 'fox in the box' kind of player, McCoist would have to do a certain level of work with his back to the opposition's goal, something which seemed to hamper him a little, and he also faced a tough opponent in the shape of big Yvon Le Roux.

Mo Johnston, 26, did not look to be quite as sharp as earlier in qualification, and he rarely got into goalscoring positions, often featuring slightly wide towards the right. Also, link-up play between the two had so far been lacking in the first 30 minutes. Still, with six qualification goals already to his name, Johnston was one of the most prolific strikers in the UEFA zone.

In the minutes following the goal, France had seen confidence return, and they were now on the front foot, passing the ball around with greater intent and looking more likely to penetrate using the two wide men. In particular, Perez looked keen, and his running down the right-hand channels was a big threat to the Scottish defence. Also, the French could now look to play counterattacks, and they often did well in the transition phases, switching from defence to attack with pace and flair. A counter on the half-hour saw Cantona play a ball towards the right -hand side of the Scottish area, where Deschamps arrived to connect first time with a volley that went straight at Leighton. He met it sweetly, but the shot did not carry enough sting to beat the number one.

While for a few minutes after their goal the hosts had been playing with their tails up, Scotland would soon regroup and looked to respond. They gradually retook the initiative, with France retreating further back and looking to exploit the visitors on the counter, and possession-wise it was now the Scots who looked to build through midfield.

There was an opportunity when a loose ball broke kindly for McCoist to the left of the area, and the striker connected first time with a sharp left-footed drive, but it hammered into the side netting. The French defenders looked a bit dumbfounded, blaming each other, and were probably disappointed to have let the Scots so close to an equalising goal with ten minutes left in the first half.

France looked sharp when they tried to catch the visitors on the break: Cantona had tried to play Perez down the right-hand channel, only for the little forward to be adjudged offside, even if it had looked like Gough had been playing him on. Scotland saw the first half out with the majority of possession, and they were looking more dangerous than before, as France dropped probably deeper than they had wanted.

With less than three minutes to go to half-time, Scotland were given a chance to equalise following the rare decision to award an indirect free kick inside the hosts' penalty area. Bats, after picking up a header back from Le Roux, had held on to the ball for too long, and referee Kurt Röthlisberger chose to penalise the keeper, presenting the Scots with a fine opportunity to grab a late first-half leveller. However, with McStay poking the ball across for MacLeod to have a pop, the Borussia Dortmund man sent a hugely disappointing shot low and wide of the upright. The five-man defensive wall had done its job. Bats, though, wanted the last word, and told the Swiss referee off for awarding the free kick in the first place, which earned him a yellow card.

France were rattled just before the break, and Scotland carved out another opportunity, this time in injury time, as MacLeod for once managed to arrive at a crossing opportunity level with the 18-yard area. He outwitted Durand to work himself into position, and though his cross took a deflection off Silvestre, he managed to find McCoist totally free in the centre. The striker looked odds-on to score with his left foot, but he guided his first-time volley against the crossbar with Bats well beaten. This was 15 seconds into time added on, and when Johnston failed to beat Éric Di Meco to the follow-up, Le Roux could eventually clear, and the referee blew the half-time whistle. It had been a very eventful few minutes right at the end, which must have given the visitors great belief that they could get something out of the game.

After those final few minutes where Scotland had come close to pulling level, France made a change during the break, with Bernard Casoni coming into the left-sided centre-back role in place of Le Roux, who added to those two earlier qualification appearances.

Scotland were looking to build on their strong finish from the opening half, though the French were stamping their authority on proceedings, stroking the ball between themselves with confidence, while the visitors tried to work out how to get close enough to the home players to force them back. France pressed well whenever the Scots were in possession, and they applied pressure higher up the pitch than had been seen during the first half. Leighton was tested by Pardo's drive from 25 yards on 49 minutes, holding on to the ball comfortably despite it bouncing a couple of yards in front of him.

After the initial high French pressure, the visitors were back on the attack themselves, and they made their first quick transition from defence to attack of their own five minutes into the second half. Malpas carried the ball at pace from inside his own half and then he found Johnston with a diagonal pass, only for the striker to fire low on the bounce with his left foot, an effort which Bats held comfortably down to his right. However, the next attempt from the Scots would be much more threatening, as the French this time made a meal of it following a long ball up from Nicol. Casoni had plenty of time to clear it, though he tried to play in Pardo, who had his back to goal and was charged down by McStay.

The midfielder's aggression set McCoist up in the area, and in turn the striker freed his partner Johnston to the right, and then ran in behind Sauzée, who tried to play offside. However, neither Casoni nor Silvestre pushed up, and McCoist was onside as he arrived inside the six-yard area, only to flick a near-post header wide of Bats's far upright. A more clean touch and the scores would've been level. It was McCoist's second close-range miss of the evening.

France had been let off the hook again; McCoist could so easily have scored. The Scottish fans were buoyed by their team's efforts, and they were quick to applaud the referee's decision to book France left-back Di Meco for a poor challenge from behind on Strachan near the halfway line on 53 minutes.

Four minutes later Di Meco was at it again, and this time he committed a similarly full-blooded tackle a few yards inside the Scottish half. His victim on this occasion was Johnston, who only realised what was coming in the fraction of a second just before Di Meco clattered into him. Johnston managed to lift his right foot, but his left foot was still rooted to the ground when he was caught by Di Meco's lunge. It was not a pretty tackle, and the red card was duly deserved. France were reduced to ten men, and they gifted the visitors a fine opportunity to get back into the game. Johnston, like Strachan before him, was able to carry on. Di Meco would now face suspension for France's final qualifier.

France had again displayed their counterattacking credentials prior to Di Meco's sending-off, when Ferreri had cut in from the left and challenged Gough along the ground. The centre-back felt he had no option but to bring the wide forward down, and the hosts had been awarded a free kick 25 yards out. It had been an opportunity for Sauzée to have a pop at goal, though he could only strike the kick into the defensive wall.

Having gone a man down, the French switched Durand from his inside-right midfield role and back into defence. This left Pardo and Deschamps pretty much to fight it out alone with their Scottish counterparts in central midfield, while Ferreri switched across to the right from his former left-sided attacking role.

At the same time, Perez moved across to the left, with Cantona still operating through the centre. It could perhaps have been interpreted just as much as a 4-2-3 as a 4-4-1. There was plenty of counterattacking ability left in the French.

Scotland would continue much in the same vein as before, but perhaps with Malpas given greater attacking freedom from his full-back position. McCoist and Johnston were occasionally switching sides up front, and both were taking some battering from the opposition's players. When Casoni was way too aggressive against McCoist on 59 minutes, it just led to another free kick.

Just after the hour mark, Andy Roxburgh told big Bayern Munich striker Alan McInally to get himself ready to come on. It did not seem out of place to think that the 26-year-old could use his aerial strength to perhaps open up more space for team-mates around him.

Before there was time to make the substitution, France increased their lead. They had once again caught the Scots on the break, although Malpas had to accept responsibility for failing to come out with the rest of the defence to play offside. Scotland were totally exposed in the centre, so when Ferreri flicked on a poor clearance from Gough, Perez's pass sent Cantona through, the forward gleefully accepting the invitation to race towards goal and finish past Leighton. Joy for the ten men, while it was a disaster for the visitors, who had shot themselves in the foot.

Scotland did eventually introduce McInally, though they had wanted to do it while just a goal down. They had to score at least twice to salvage a point, and making way for the striker was Strachan. The right-sided midfielder had not always stuck to his position, and the Scots had not too often made inroads down the right. Even full-back Nicol had been reluctant to trot forward, and in taking off their designated

Scotland line up ahead of the match game against West Germany at the 1986 FIFA World Cup

1986 World Cup: Gordon Strachan scores v West Germany to give Scotland a shock lead in Querétaro

Jim Leighton gathers the ball under pressure from Peter Beardsley in a home international against England in 1988

Richard Gough on the ball at Wembley in the same game

Gary Mackay lines up ahead of the last of his four caps for Scotland

Murdo MacLeod in action against England at Wembley in 1988

Gordon Durie scores in Yugoslavia in a World Cup qualifying match in Zagreb in September 1989

Ally McCoist scores past Erik Thorstvedt of Norway in November 1989 …

… and celebrates the goal in the 1-1 draw

Paul McStay during Scotland's 2-1 win over Cyprus at Hampden in April 1989

Roy Aitken in action at Hampden Park in 1990

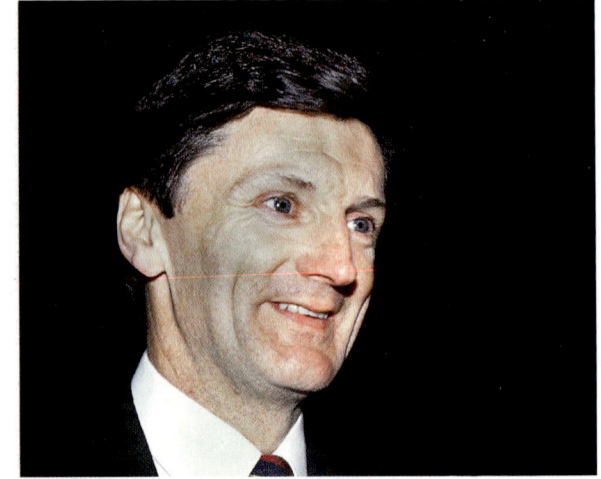

Andy Roxburgh is all smiles after Scotland qualify for the 1990 World Cup

Jim Bett outpaces Ismail Youssef of Egypt, as Scotland warm up for Italia 90 in May of that year

Dave McPherson wins a tackle against Costa Rica at the 1990 World Cup

Alex McLeish challenges Stefan Pettersson in Scotland's 2-1 win over Sweden at Italia 90 …

… Gordon Durie battles with Tomas Brolin as Scotland take on Sweden in Genoa …

… Robert Fleck in action in the same game

Mo Johnston scores the crucial second goal against Sweden from the penalty spot

Jim Leighton in despair against Brazil as Scotland crash out of the World Cup

Mo Johnston in action for Scotland against Brazil in 1990

right-sided player, McInally took up his position as a centre-forward, with Johnston and McCoist feeding off him.

The idea was that MacLeod would work as a third midfielder alongside Aitken and McStay, although he would still not forget about his original left-sided position. They may have been enjoying the majority of possession, but the introduction of a target man had not yielded further attempts at goal, and McInally even appeared to the right among the front three rather than in the centre.

It seemed a waste to have McInally on at all if Scotland were not playing to his strengths. In midfield, McStay at times was indecisive, while Aitken was the one motoring up the pitch. From the back, Nicol appeared to be the one hoisting the ball forward.

Roxburgh could see that pulling a goal back didn't look imminent, and in the wake of a yellow card for McLeish following a juicy tackle from behind on Cantona, he introduced his second substitute as, on 76 minutes, Aberdeen midfielder Jim Bett replaced the ineffective MacLeod. So both the Scottish wide men were off; Bett's only qualification appearance had come wide to the left in midfield in the 1-1 home draw with Yugoslavia, and he had left a very poor impression. Now, the stockily built 29-year-old would slot into the central position of their three-man midfield, with McStay to his right and Aitken to his left. At club level, Bett was known for his playmaking ability, and now was the time for him to show that for the national team.

The French were unaffected by the latest Scottish changes, and they continued to play with assuredness throughout their team, despite the fact that they were a man down. Their defence was unmoved by the entrance of McInally, with Sauzée and Casoni well in control. Durand was mobile along the left, and not afraid to venture inside the Scotland half. Pardo and Deschamps continued to display their midfield aggression, rarely giving the Scottish players any time on the ball. And the front three kept pinning back the visitors' defence, as there was still plenty of running left in their legs. The fact that Ferreri and Perez had switched sides did not appear to have reduced France's threat levels, and the clever positioning of Cantona seemed to complement the two wide forwards well.

There was to be no final Scottish onslaught; it never came off. Instead, some of their players were visibly upset, and surely no one more so than captain Aitken. The Celtic man repeatedly showed his disgust, probably just as much with his own performance as the scoreline. However, a bad night was about to take a turn for the worse, and it was yet another French counter for the final goal of the evening: Ferreri was the architect as he found substitute Bravo with a right-wing cross, which was headed out by Nicol for a corner on the right. Gough could only get a faint header away from Ferreri's kick, and the ball fell into the path of Durand, who collected on the edge of the area. He sidestepped Gough with a Cruyff turn, before he shot low, left-footed via Nicol and into the back of the net for 3-0. It was game over, and the hosts could rejoice.

Scotland had started well but they failed to produce opportunities before they suddenly fell behind on 26 minutes following some disappointing defending to allow Deschamps to strike home. An inspired French team looked to sit back and allow the visitors to have the majority of possession, and hit the somewhat sluggish Scots on the break.

It was not a bad tactic, even if they were fortunate to preserve their lead through to half-time with McCoist hitting the bar in first-half injury time. It had not been a part of the plan to have left-back Di Meco sent off early in the second half, after McCoist had given the hosts another scare with a header, though Scotland failed to take advantage of being a man up, and again they were exposed defensively as Cantona was played onside by Malpas to finish one-on-one with Leighton.

Even a switch to 4-3-3 failed to ignite the visitors, and France wrapped up their win with a somewhat fortuitous deflected goal from Durand a minute from full time.

The defeat did not dampen the spirits of students Simon Rioch, Paul Ross and Kenny Thompson from Glasgow. Simon recalled, 'We went over on a flight from Glasgow on the morning of the game. It was our first time in Paris and the game was a wee bit of a blur. We didn't play badly, but Leighton was poor again.'

Kenny added, 'We did all right for about an hour but Cantona was superb.'

And Paul looked back, 'To be honest, it was more of a lads' trip than to watch Scotland, but we had loads of supporters at the ground. We were in good voice but once France took the lead we never looked like coming back. I never liked that away kit. We should have scored after they had a man sent off but we were too predictable. I think Roxburgh had set them up for a draw and when they took the lead they ran away with it.'

The final scoreline did not tell the whole story. Scotland had played well in patches and could have scored one or two goals. It was particularly disappointing that when France went down to ten men, the Scots failed to take advantage and at least pull a goal back. They seemed to lack belief when they went 2-0 down.

Richard Gough looked comfortable at centre-back alongside Alex McLeish, but once again it was the midfield where the Scots looked vulnerable. Gordon Strachan failed to have any impact, rarely getting to the byline, and producing few crosses. Roy Aitken and Paul McStay battled hard but toiled against the quicker and more skilful French midfield. Aitken was too slow and although a good leader and skipper, he lacked the mobility to be an effective defensive midfielder.

He was strong but needed quicker and more skilful players alongside him to do his running. McStay was a talented player and the two Celtic men always worked hard. However, they did not play alongside each other at club level, as Aitken played at centre-back for his club.

Roxburgh had tried numerous different players in wide positions, but seemed to favour solid, more defensive players who could tuck in when Scotland were out of possession. Steve Nicol was his preferred choice, as he could play wide right or wide left. Murdo MacLeod was steady enough and Roxburgh valued his European experience with Dortmund. Up front, former Nantes striker Mo Johnston could find no way past a resolute French defence, but Ally McCoist looked sharp and dangerous throughout. So it would all come down to the final game at home to Norway.

13

Hampden Heroes – Italy Here We Come

15 November 1989 – Scotland 1 Norway 1

SINCE SUCCESSIVE away defeats to Yugoslavia and France had put in question Scotland's World Cup participation, this was their chance to put the record straight: avoid defeat and they were off to Italy. Scotland had a two-point advantage over France, but with the latter's final game coming up three days later, the Scots would have to expect Cyprus to return empty-handed from Paris, so if they did their bit, they were through no matter what. They had overcome the Norwegians in their opening qualifier, 2-1 in Oslo, and with the visitors having little but pride to play for, another win for Scotland, who were strong on home soil, with two wins and that draw against Yugoslavia so far in the campaign, seemed likely.

With just that solitary point required, Andy Roxburgh needed to put faith in some players who had so far been peripheral in the qualifiers. The matchday programme had listed 18 players, but there was ultimately no space in the final squad of 16 for either of Steve Nicol, of Liverpool,

133

who was injured, or Everton's Stuart McCall, who had not featured in any of the qualifiers so far.

Scotland had three ever-presents in defenders Maurice Malpas and Alex McLeish, and midfielder Paul McStay. The latter had started the qualification brilliantly, but had perhaps faded somewhat. Scotland had shipped six goals from their two previous qualifiers, losing in Yugoslavia and France, and perhaps they were not overly confident coming into this fixture. Eight of the players who had started in the 2-1 win in Oslo were still available to Roxburgh. Their greatest loss was perhaps Richard Gough, who had performed admirably in the right-back position in four out of six previous qualifiers, and in the centre of defence in the defeat in Paris. On a more positive note, they would welcome back Willie Miller, who had missed out on the trip to France.

An interesting, if surprising, inclusion was left-winger Davie Cooper, a veteran aged 33. He was famous for his 12-year career with Rangers, but had switched to Motherwell at the start of the season. Scotland had struggled to identify the ideal man for the left-wing berth, though two and a half years had passed since Cooper's previous cap. Was his return a hint of desperation by Roxburgh? Pat Nevin was also available, capable of performing on either flank. His one appearance in qualification so far had come in the 2-1 home win against Cyprus.

Norway had been in Kuwait towards the end of October, and in a friendly against the hosts they'd drawn 2-2, seeing two young midfielders in Dag Riisnæs and Lars Bohinen make their debuts. In addition to that, Frigg midfielder Bent Skammelsrud had won only his second cap. All three were included for the trip to Glasgow. This left out players such as Sverre Brandhaug, Ørjan Berg and Kjetil Osvold, who had all played substantial roles in Norway's bid to reach the finals.

Add to that the absence of Jahn Ivar Jakobsen through suspension after two yellow cards, the left-sided man who had enjoyed some fine performances recently, and also regular right-sided midfielder Karl Petter Løken, so some major changes were unavoidable.

Barring an unlikely slip-up from France at home to Cyprus, Norway would finish fourth in the table regardless of the outcome here. So they could play without a whole lot of pressure. Scotland lined up with:

Leighton
McPherson–Miller (MacLeod 63)–McLeish–Malpas
Aitken (c)–Bett–McStay–Cooper (McClair 74)
Johnston–McCoist

Norway kicked off through their front pair of Jan Åge Fjørtoft and Gøran Sørloth. For the hosts, there were starting roles for defender Dave McPherson, who had played at centre-half in his one qualifier so far, the home game against Cyprus, and wide man Davie Cooper, who had got the nod ahead of a player like Murdo MacLeod. There was also a second start in qualification for Jim Bett, Aberdeen's skilful midfielder. The highly experienced Willie Miller was back at the heart of the defence alongside his Aberdeen compatriot Alex McLeish, who had played every single minute of the fixtures so far.

In the Norwegian camp, there were a few expected changes. Big defender Erland Johnsen had come into the side, but also playing were Terje Kojedal and Rune Bratseth, so they looked to have reverted to a strong three-man central defensive unit. They had not played with five at the back since losing 3-0 at home to Poland in a May friendly.

That had spelled the end of a six-game run using three centre-backs, in which they'd shipped 13 goals. As expected, Hugo Hansen slotted in at right-back, while Skammelsrud got his starting role in midfield, possibly as the inside-left, and there was also just a second start of the campaign for Tom Gulbrandsen, with the inside-right role reserved for him.

In the early stages Scotland took the game to the visitors. They swarmed around the Norwegians in midfield, looking to release their strikers early, and were pressing all around the park. The Scots were playing with energy, passion and determination. The early proceedings were much more reminiscent of Scotland's form from early in the campaign, rather than the team which had been stuttering since the turn of the year.

There was a high level of anticipation in the air. The Hampden Park terraces did their bit to cheer on their heroes, regularly singing 'Flower of Scotland' and also 'Que será, será, whatever will be, will be, we're going to Italy, que será, será'

While Scotland started the game on the front foot, throwing themselves into tackles, keeping pace and always looking for a team-mate in an advanced position, this Norwegian team could be something of an unpredictable force. Even though they'd lost four out of their seven qualifiers, there was certainly quality within their ranks, even if the 11 as a whole had often failed to perform. They would really need to raise their game to get anything from Scotland on such an important occasion.

The away side cast their usual 4-4-2 formation aside for this match, returning to the 5-3-2 which their team selection had hinted at before kick-off. Norway had been lined up with the traditional four-man defensive line in their home defeat against Scotland but had switched to five at the back for their trip to Paris just two weeks after. They would continue like that through the winter, but once summer had returned to their shores, manager Ingvar Stadheim had opted for the familiar and trusted 4-4-2 once again for the visit of Cyprus. Their three-man central defensive unit on this occasion mirrored the one which had appeared during that 1-0 loss in France nearly 14 months earlier, although there was a slight alteration in their formation.

Despite the Scottish grit and passion, Norway did not buckle early on, and they looked to find their feet and try to build up some kind of passing rhythm of their own. However, this was where they struggled, as they looked woefully inept in midfield, where two of their three men certainly were playing with nerves. The calm and composed head of Per Egil Ahlsen at the heart of their midfield three had really given the Norwegians composure since coming into the side for their final three qualifiers, but around him were the erratic Gulbrandsen and an international novice in Skammelsrud.

The early Scottish midfield superiority made it very difficult for a Norway team lacking in pace, due to the absence of industrious wide-left player Jakobsen, and they were not able to build any kind of pattern themselves. They tried to play it into the feet of Sørloth and Fjørtoft up front for the two to hold on to the ball and bring others into play, but they struggled to retain possession.

One player who Norway had relied on right through the qualification had been Erik Thorstvedt. The big Tottenham goalkeeper had overcome a difficult start to his career in England to begin building a sound reputation, although he failed twice to collect crosses in quick succession, leading to some frantic defending by the visitors. Luckily for Thorstvedt, Bratseth was able to scramble the ball clear and the visitors could eventually breathe more easily again. Thorstvedt had turned 27 at the end of October, and this was his 57th international appearance; he did not lack experience of high balls and direct football.

In midfield for Norway, Hansen seemed more technically equipped than Gunnar Halle – at the time of Lillestrøm but later to play in England with Oldham, Leeds, Bradford and Wolverhampton Wanderers – displaying some nice sidesteps on two separate occasions, and with some midfielders unable to hold on to the ball, Hansen's capability to do so was even more important.

To the left in defence, the Norwegians had teenage full-back Stig Inge Bjørnebye, who was featuring for a third successive qualifier, and who so far had looked very accomplished. Bjørnebye was enthusiastic, he played with plenty of energy and he was strong in the tackle. Despite his tender years, he did not seem to be overawed by any occasion, as journeys to Yugoslavia and now Scotland had proved. He was also willing to cross the halfway line, and he possessed a particularly fine left foot with which he could swing deliveries into the penalty area.

Bjørnebye was also capable in the air, and it did look as if in him Norway would have a fine left-sided defender for years to come. He had shown no fear in combatting Dragan Stojković in Sarajevo, and now, up against the highly experienced Scottish captain Roy Aitken, he once again acquitted himself well, keeping hold of the ball and not allowing Aitken to intimidate him.

Norway's central defensive unit seemed perhaps their strongest attribute. Captaining them was one of West German Bundesliga's finest liberos in 28-year-old Rune Bratseth, whose international reputation kept growing. He had been Norway's libero throughout the qualification, and seemed at ease whether he was playing in a four- or five-man defensive line. On this occasion, though, Stadheim had put his captain as their left-sided centre-back, with their most experienced team member inside of him in the central one among the three roles: Terje Kojedal.

Kojedal was a typical hard-as-nails player, though he also had fine ability with the ball at his feet. Just as much as Bratseth, he was more likely to venture forward and into enemy territory, particularly comfortable when looking to pass the ball cleverly with his left foot. The 32-year-old had been one of Norway's more consistent performers right through their qualification fixtures.

To complement Bratseth and Kojedal at the back was another physically imposing player: Erland Johnsen. The 22-year-old flame-haired centre-back was only sparingly used by his club, Bayern Munich, but he was learning from capable defensive authorities such as Klaus Augenthaler and Hans Pflügler, and on this occasion Johnsen was working to the right among their three-man unit.

While he did not have the same level of ability in terms of positioning or tactical awareness as the other two, Johnsen held absolutely no fear, and he would give as good as he got in any battle with the Scottish strikers. Physically, the visitors appeared well prepared to tackle the hosts.

In the Scottish back line, there was the return of 34-year-old campaigner Willie Miller, who had captained his country several times, even once in qualification, the home draw against Yugoslavia. Miller had been suffering with a recurring knee injury over the past year and a half, which saw him miss various matches at both club and international level.

Paired alongside him was his Aberdeen team-mate Alex McLeish, who had captained the team at home to France. Andy Roxburgh could not have asked for a pair with greater international know-how for such a crucial fixture. While this was McLeish's 66th appearance in a Scotland shirt, it was Miller's 65th.

Miller swept, while McLeish was typically thrust into challenges with either of the two Norwegian strikers. They looked to be marking zonally, though McLeish was once again operating as the left-sided centre-half. While McLeish would come up for attacking set pieces, Miller would remain back. Speed was no longer Miller's forte, but his reading of the game and positional sense still made him a big asset to the side.

Scotland were without the marauding right-back Richard Gough. He had been one of their best and more consistent performers throughout the qualification, and was a hugely important player at set pieces at both ends of the pitch. Replacing the Stockholm-born defender was Hearts' giant centre-back Dave McPherson, who slotted into the right-back position.

This was McPherson's second appearance of the qualification, to add to his outing at centre-back during the 2-1 home win against Cyprus in April. Due to his sheer size, he was a huge asset in the air, though he did not seem as comfortable in coming forward as the player he had replaced.

To the left in defence, Scotland had one of their more reliable performers in the two-footed Maurice Malpas. The Dundee United defender had been a vital part of the national team for four years, and was a calm and collected left-back. It was quite noticeable how he would use either foot in passing or crossing and he was more than capable of coming forward to assist inside the opposition's half. Roxburgh wanted width from his full-backs, and Malpas was clearly a more natural player coming forward than McPherson, who was much more comfortable in central defence.

The first meaningful attack of the game came just after the 17-minute mark. Norway had been trying to build up patiently, playing it into the feet of Sørloth, who in turn would bring Hansen into play down the right. However, the full-back lost possession and Scotland could mount a quality counterattack. Jim Bett took the ball in the centre of the pitch, spotting Mo Johnston making a fine run to his left.

Johnston got the ball, took it inside and eventually found Ally McCoist, via a little flick from Bett. McCoist had his back to goal inside the area, and rather than taking an extra touch to compose himself, he spun quickly and fired a half-hearted left-footed effort straight into the arms of Thorstvedt from 15 yards.

As the first half approached the halfway stage, Norway were seemingly coming into it a little more. They had managed to push higher up the pitch and the frenetic Scottish pressure in midfield had started to relent. With the game evenly balanced at 0-0, the relative silence from the capacity crowd told a tale of a nerve-racked stadium. Norway had at a left-wing corner from which Hansen's deep cross to the far side of the area was headed away by Aitken, though Ahlsen failed to capitalise as the ball went straight into Leighton's arms.

In midfield, Norway were numerically superior than their hosts, by three men to two, even if one of their centre-backs would occasionally push forward, contributing to an even greater advantage. This meant that Scotland tucked their right-sided midfielder more inside, something that Aitken found quite natural anyway. The two inside midfielders for the visitors, Gulbrandsen and Skammelsrud, had so far failed to raise their game from their early struggles, and they continued to play peripheral roles, with Ahlsen and one from Bratseth or Kojedal taking control of possession.

Ahlsen, of Brann, had, like Bjørnebye, come into the side for their final three qualifiers, and his composure appeared to be his greatest asset. He was 31 so did not have the legs to not carry him with great speed, but he had a fine footballing brain, with good awareness of players around him.. He compensated well for his slow feet with his ability to distribute the ball. Ahlsen was also a set-piece taker, and quite instrumental in the team.

To Ahlsen's left was 23-year-old Bent Skammelsrud, making his third international appearance. He plied his trade in the Norwegian second tier with ambitious Oslo club Frigg. He seemed very lightweight, and also appeared to be intimidated by some of his physically imposing opponents. In the space of seven minutes midway through the first half, he went to ground on three separate occasions, after challenges from McPherson, McStay and Aitken, and after the latter, he stayed down in need of treatment

Across from Skammelsrud was Lillestrøm's Tom Gulbrandsen, making his sixth squad appearance of the qualification campaign, though only his second start. He had come on for the last few minutes as well as being a non-appearing substitute in Yugoslavia. Gulbrandsen, 25, seemed to prefer chasing the ball rather than being in possession, and so far seemed very uncomfortable with the ball at feet. The visitors failed to keep possession in the centre of the park, although Ahlsen, Bratseth and Kojedal were all capable ball players.

The Scottish midfield had four players, but those who had been expecting to see the usual Aitken-McStay partnership in the centre would be disappointed. Roxburgh had once again included the pair in his starting 11, as per norm in this qualification: both would start for an eighth successive time. While McStay had stayed on the pitch for the full 90 minutes in every game, Aitken had come off during the second half in both of their first two.

Aitken, closing in on his 31st birthday, was making his 50th appearance for Scotland. He was a key player of great experience and had fine battling qualities; he was one of the first names on the manager's team sheet. Aitken had begun in the centre alongside his Celtic mate McStay in each of their seven qualifiers so far, though on this occasion he had been shifted out to the right.

Scotland had at times struggled for width, perhaps particularly along the left, though with skipper Aitken the crowd were unlikely to see a player constantly hitting the byline to put crosses in. Even if he did his best to maintain width along the right, particularly in possession, he would struggle to make any great runs down the right, instead opting to hit a cross from a deeper position. Defensively, he would tuck inside when the visitors were in possession, giving the hosts a numerical midfield advantage. Roxburgh could not have asked for more in a leader and captain and for the commitment which he would always get from Aitken. It should be noted that he had featured wide on the right of midfield also in the 1989 Scottish Cup Final, when Celtic had won by the only goal of the game against arch rivals Rangers.

McStay had begun the campaign brilliantly, accepting a lot of responsibility in the centre of the park, and he'd even scored the winning goal in Norway. He was sound in possession, and he would often look to make forward passes to feet and looked particularly at home when he could burst into the area. He had only recently turned 25, but this was already McStay's 41st cap.

Alongside the Celtic man on this occasion was Aberdeen's Jim Bett. The powerfully built 29-year-old had only played a bit-part role so far in the qualification, coming off in the second half in the home draw against Yugoslavia, and then coming on during the heavy defeat in France, where he had gone into the central midfield role in Scotland's late push in a 4-3-3 formation.

The Dons fans loved him, though, and he certainly appeared to be more at home in the centre of the pitch. Bett would be the one player who the others would look to for possession, and he was more of a playmaker. He was, like Malpas, very good with both feet, and he had plenty of energy alongside the enthusiastic McStay.

Scotland had held the upper hand in the first 15 minutes or so, and there was cause to believe that Bett and McStay would continue to dominate in the heart of the pitch. While Murdo MacLeod had occupied the left-sided midfield position for the two successive away defeats, Scotland had failed to identify their ideal man for this role. MacLeod had been the sixth player in six matches to feature there, and now, through the return of Davie Cooper, Roxburgh had a seventh player in eight qualifiers to perform along the left. Cooper, a genius during his Rangers days, had not played for the national team since a 2-0 home defeat against Brazil in 1987. He would bring width to the team, and Scotland would often look to build down the left. His understanding with Malpas behind him did not always seem strong as they tried to get more and more into the game.

Both teams featured two strikers. For the hosts, Roxburgh had once again gone with the trusted duo of Mo Johnston and Ally McCoist, both now also working together at club level for Rangers after Johnston's stint in French football with Nantes.

Johnston had set off like a whirlwind, scoring six goals in the first five qualifiers, though he'd failed to score since, despite not travelling to Zagreb for the Yugoslavia game due to injury. As for McCoist, he'd been a bit unlucky so far, although he did have one goal in Scotland's last five qualifiers.

Whereas McCoist was a natural poacher through the centre, you would often see more movement from Johnston, who would regularly run into the channels or even out wide. It was from such a position that Johnston would carve out the best opportunity of the match so far. On 24 minutes he accepted Cooper's pass in the left-hand channel, running towards the byline before hitting a low cross into the centre for McCoist to connect with his right foot. The effort from point-blank range was scrambled away from goal by Thorstvedt's leg, denying a certain goal.

For the visitors, 22-year-old Jan Åge Fjørtoft was making his sixth start, alongside the 27-year-old Gøran

Sørloth. They had scored two and three goals during the qualification respectively, though Fjørtoft seemed the more enthusiastic of the two, certainly in terms of his movement. Sørloth would at times play with his back to goal, being the target for high balls up from the back, although he was not particularly tall for a centre-forward. He did look to have fine vision, though, and was good at bringing others into play.

Fjørtoft was typically the one making runs into the channels, and while he had often been appearing towards left-sided areas as long as Jakobsen was a feature in the team, he was now working more towards the right with Jakobsen out, thus bringing him into battles with McLeish. The pair had coincidentally met in that season's UEFA Cup, when Rapid Vienna had knocked Aberdeen out in the first round on the away goals rule. Fjørtoft had struck the only goal in the meeting in the Austrian capital.

There were not a whole lot of natural pauses in the first half, and the pace had been picking up again after a few minutes when the hosts had no longer been quite as intense with their pressing. Right on the half-hour, there was another big chance for McCoist to put Scotland ahead. He seized on a poor mistake by Sørloth on the near post as he failed to clear Cooper's free kick from the left. McCoist didn't have much time to react, but he prodded goalwards, forcing another save by Thorstvedt from close range. It seemed just a matter of time before Scotland broke the deadlock.

With nothing much to show for in an attacking sense so far in the game, Norway carved out two efforts within the space of 30 seconds. They had a free kick near the halfway line, which was hit towards the edge of the area by Hansen.

Skammelsrud managed to get his head to the ball, with McLeish arriving late for the challenge, and it dropped down in the area, bouncing awkwardly for McPherson, who had Sørloth right behind him. With Leighton coming off his line to try and claim, McPherson headed back to his keeper from close range, which gave Sørloth an opportunity to react by getting to the rebound. Leighton was off his line, but McPherson got the block in to deny Sørloth, and the Scots were able to clear their lines. Moments later, Fjørtoft got the ball after a poor attempt from Malpas to head clear, and he spun and fired just over goal from inside the area. Despite the nerves and the occasion, it had been an enthralling game.

The half seemed to be petering out with no goals to show for it, even if the hosts had made a few fine opportunities, notably through McCoist. The two Scottish strikers were working tirelessly off the ball, making fine runs to try and unsettle the three-man Norwegian central defensive unit, and it would ultimately pay dividends right before the whistle. A Thorstvedt punt downfield was headed back into space by Malpas. McCoist made a clever run in behind Bratseth, which saw him arrive first to the ball after it had bounced twice. Thorstvedt had come racing out from his area, but was beaten to it by McCoist, who lobbed the ball over him and into the back of the net, sparking some wild celebrations among players and fans alike. It was a great strike and, as the players celebrated, Andy Roxburgh jumped up to celebrate with the bench.

Polish referee Michał Listkiewicz, who was having a fine game, blew his whistle for half-time a minute into time added on, as there had been on-pitch treatment for Skammelsrud and Aitken. Other than that, there had been few stoppages.

Scotland had a deserved lead at the break, though with a huge final 45 minutes to come. Any French fans watching from the comfort of their homes or listening in would not have been best pleased about that goal right on the stroke of 45 minutes, making their own task of qualifying an impossible one, although two Norway goals in the second half would change all that. The goal, incidentally, was McCoist's fifth for Scotland on his 19th appearance.

The second half started off a bit cagily, with neither side willing to throw men forward. As the game wore on the pace increased. Norway continued in their 5-3-2, reluctant to immediately give up on their defensive security, and the hosts were also unchanged in how they lined up.

It was noticeable that the Scottish midfield had the upper hand, despite their numerical disadvantage, as McStay and particularly Bett were doing their utmost to put pressure on their opponents when Norway were in possession or to maintain the pace in their passing game when the Scots were on the ball.

There had been a couple of times during the first half when Norway had lost the ball before they could break out of their own half, either due to sloppy passing or because the Scottish pressure was so intense, and this would happen again eight minutes into the second half. Kojedal, who had so far probably looked like their most assured defensive player in possession, played it straight to McStay. The midfield man accepted the invitation and immediately headed for the byline. He attempted a low cross into the feet of McCoist, but luckily for the visitors, Bratseth was again well positioned to cut the ball out and give away a Scotland corner.

A couple of minutes earlier, some interpassing between Cooper and Bett had led to the latter setting Dave McPherson up for a shooting chance from 25 yards. The right-back struck it well but the ball flew a yard over the bar. The Norwegians were still not engaging their midfield a whole lot, rather just playing it quickly in the direction of either striker, or just using their wide defenders getting forward, with both Hansen and Bjørnebye keen to support the attack. Among their midfield three, Ahlsen continued to give the best impression, as he sat in the centre and acted very composed every time he was played into possession.

Skammelsrud looked like a passenger and had contributed little. Gulbrandsen still displayed his peculiar running style, and he had the first clear shooting opportunity after the break as the ball dropped kindly for him on the edge of the area. He struck it well on the half-volley but he failed to keep the shot down and it flew over, with Leighton scrambling across. It would've been a screamer had it gone in, and it would've come from a very unlikely source too.

Scotland went desperately close to increasing their advantage on 57 minutes. Cooper used his precise left foot to cross into the box. The ball evaded McCoist and Hansen on the near post, only to strike Johnsen on the edge of the six-yard area, to the right in the centre. It cannoned off the defender and went over via the crossbar with Thorstvedt beaten. Johnsen was able to breathe a big sigh of relief, but would those missed chances come back to haunt Scotland? Andy Roxburgh knew that a one-goal lead would not be enough to kill off the Norwegians.

Both teams had players warming up along the touchline early in the second half, with Murdo MacLeod for Scotland and Lars Bohinen for the visitors hoping to come on. With no truly recognised defender among their substitutes, the Scots would be looking to MacLeod for defensive cover, even if the original idea might have been him replacing Cooper on the wing. Cooper was not having a poor match, but he was also not exerting much influence, even if it had been his free kick that had been headed on to his own goal frame by Johnsen. In open play, Cooper didn't seem to have the pace to get into good positions for delivery.

However, cruel luck would have it that Willie Miller would go to ground after an accidental clash with Norway's Hansen well inside Scottish territory after Fjørtoft had tried to release the full-back with a crossfield pass. Miller had got to the ball a fraction of a second before Hansen, who had then caught the ageing defender with his knee. Miller looked to have had his studs caught in the grass, twisting his knee and injuring his ligaments. It looked painful when he was being attended to by physio Hugh Allan, although Miller would dust himself off and continue.

Sadly, it was clear he was in agony, and the eventual substitution was inevitable, even if it only took place nine minutes after the incident with Hansen. Miller had long since been struggling with his knees, and this had hardly made his situation any better. It was a blow for Roxburgh to lose such an experienced defender.

The visitors made the first change, though, as the luckless Skammelsrud came off for Bohinen, with the substitute also making his qualification debut three weeks after his first international appearance, during a 2-2 friendly in Kuwait. It turned out to be a straight swap, with Skammelsrud looking out of his depth. Bohinen, 20, looked raw, but he seemed to play with more enthusiasm and he would add some further energy to their midfield.

On 62 minutes, Scotland once again came desperately close to increasing their lead. Cooper had played a low cross from a deep position along the left, and it had evaded everybody until McCoist picked it up to the right of centre. He took a touch to improve his angle, and seemed to be tripped by a combination of Bjørnebye and Bratseth just inside the area as he was trying to steady himself. The ball broke for Johnston who hit it low first time with his right foot, only to see big Thorstvedt dive down and get enough of a palm to it to just turn it beyond the upright and away for a corner. It was a big opportunity, and the visitors could once again thank their in-form-keeper for keeping them in the game.

A minute and a half after Thorstvedt's save, Fjørtoft went mightily close down the other end. The lively striker had been played in by Kojedal, and with Miller still feeling the effects of the hit to his right knee, backing off him, he could take a few steps inside from the left-hand channel and let fly from 25 yards. The shot didn't carry a lot of power, but Fjørtoft had gone for precision, and he would strike it low against the upright with Leighton beaten, the ball cannoning off the post and back into play, and the Scottish defence scrambled the ball clear.

Fjørtoft looked to have more or less switched sides with Sørloth in the second half, with the latter now appearing more towards the right, and Fjørtoft operating in more familiar central-left areas.

With Miller clearly unable to continue, Scotland struggled to get the substitution made as Norway piled on the pressure, and the ball did not exit play for several minutes. Only when Leighton had the ball played back to him by Malpas could it be kicked out. Miller would finally hobble off midway through the half, and he was replaced by MacLeod.

While this did not appear to be a like-for-like replacement, MacLeod had been featuring as a libero on several occasions for his club side Borussia Dortmund in West Germany. MacLeod didn't instinctively seem to be a fit as a withdrawn, right-sided centre-half, but that was where he slotted in, and his years of experience at club and international levels would stand him in good stead. So McLeish would be the one who first and foremost challenged the Norwegian strikers, and it would be Sørloth coming into the rock-solid centre-back's territory the most, while MacLeod would look to instigate from the back.

Scotland created another fine opportunity on 72 minutes, much of it due to the perseverance of Maurice Malpas, who was having a very sound game at left-back. He won a challenge for the ball with Hansen 15 yards inside the Norwegian half after a crossfield pass from Fjørtoft, and then he went on to beat Johnsen in another 50/50 challenge. He managed to get to the byline and fling in a cross from the left. He hit it low towards the edge of the area, where Johnston met it with an outstretched leg, yet again forcing Thorstvedt into action: the keeper managed to throw himself to his left once more, and this time he held on to the ball. The big Spurs stopper really earned his wages on this performance; on another day the Scots could have scored two or three more goals.

There was a third player substitution of the evening when the hosts opted to withdraw Davie Cooper after his return to the national team. It had been likely that he'd have been substituted for MacLeod earlier had Miller's injury not occurred, though on 74 minutes the ageing wing man's time was up. It had been a decent comeback by Cooper, who was replaced by Manchester United's Brian McClair. The 25-year-old former Celtic man had enjoyed a fine second half in midfield during Scotland's earlier win in Oslo, and was thrust into the midfield once again this time, albeit towards the left rather than as the most advanced player in a diamond. Roxburgh then decided to swap positions for Aitken and Bett, to shore things up defensively.

Not a lot was happening in terms of action at either end of the pitch in the ensuing few minutes. The Scots were clearly content with what they'd got, and they played with caution, seeing McClair tuck in from his left-sided midfield position, something which made them lose width along that flank. Opposite from him, Bett had gone slightly anonymous on the right; being less involved appeared not to suit him. McStay had definitely shown glimpses of his undoubted quality, but all in all he also had more of an average kind of game, probably outshone by Bett. Aitken moved into the left side of the central area, and was sitting relatively deep as Scotland tried to hold on to their lead.

There was not much adventure left in the hosts at this stage. McClair's crossfield run to try and reach McPherson's ball up from the right-back position resulted in him accidentally scything Kojedal down, something which resulted in the big defender having to go off with a thigh injury.

The home fans were buoyant as they realised just how close Scotland now were to making it through to a fifth successive World Cup. The noise levels inside Hampden Park were massive, and while there had been further renditions of 'Flower of Scotland' earlier, the supporters were now just building up towards a crescendo of sound. There was little from the Norwegians in attack to pose much of a threat to the slender Scottish lead. When Hansen misplaced a pass straight into the feet of McClair, the hosts launched a counterattack with just two minutes left on the clock. McClair fed Johnston to the left and then made a run through the centre, where the visitors were exposed, as both Johnsen and Bratseth were inside the Scottish half. McClair received a return pass from Johnston, and while all he really needed to do was dart past Bjørnebye, he decided to pass it inside to the onrushing Aitken.

This took the sting out of the ball and ultimately Thorstvedt could gather a poor cross from the right. When referee Listkiewicz blew for a foul from McCoist on Johnsen just inside the Norwegian half of the pitch a minute into time added on, the home fans thought for a moment this was the final whistle. However, there were still a few seconds left, still sufficient time for Norway to hit an unlikely equaliser, and it would even happen through the most unlikely of sources. Fjørtoft's strike against the post earlier in the half apart, they had failed to build much attacking momentum, and Scotland's 1-0 lead had not looked threatened inside the final few minutes.

Once Bohinen had passed the ball sideways, through the legs of McStay a few yards inside the Scottish half, Johnsen arrived and, for whatever, reason opted to shoot from 45 yards. While it had been an inexplicable decision to do so in the first place, what happened next was even more of a mystery, with Leighton fumbling the ball over the goal line and into the back of the net. Norway had an equaliser, something which completely stunned everyone present, with Hampden Park going silent. If the French were watching, they could be forgiven for eyeing a late opportunity for a Norwegian comeback win.

It wasn't to be, however, as the game barely had time to restart before it was all over. Leighton had time to pick up a McClair back pass and that was it, two minutes into stoppage time. It was time for Hampden Park to erupt with emotions, as the fans could finally celebrate World Cup qualification. Scotland 1 Norway 1 – a fifth World Cup in a row.

Scotland had dominated the first half, using their physique and tempo, unsettling the visitors. However, Thorstvedt was in irresistible mood, and saved two close-range efforts from danger man McCoist. Right on the stroke of half-time, though, it was the Scottish striker who had the last laugh, as he latched on to a Malpas header to lob beyond the keeper and into the back of the net. Scotland still created chances after the break, but again the big man between the sticks kept the score down. At the other end, Fjørtoft saw a shot from distance cannon off the post. The hosts appeared to be heading for a deserved 1-0 win when Johnsen popped up with an unlikely effort from 45 yards in the second minute of time added on.

It was a howler by Leighton but no one inside the stadium cared with the final whistle sounding shortly after: Scotland were through to Italia 90. Cue celebrations in the streets of Glasgow and all around Scotland.

Post-match, Andy Roxburgh told ITV's Brian Moore of his reaction to qualifying, 'Relief, one word. We are just happy to be through to the World Cup finals. It was always going to be agony, a game like this for us. We remember well playing against Bulgaria in Bulgaria when they needed a draw to get through to the European finals, and we went there and won 1-0, simply because the nerves got to them. Now you could see tonight a lot of our players didn't play as well as they can, they definitely were nervous, inevitably in the environment they were playing in. And Alistair McCoist had opened the scoring for us and their goalkeeper did very well on occasion I mean we should have been more than one up and the game was won.

'And then suddenly this rocket went flying into the back of the net and we were all panicking. We were just hoping that the referee didn't have the East German elastic watch, and we were just happy it finished the way it did and we were through.

'The key factors were just about attitude really. It was not the kind of performance that we would normally like to put on as I say it was far too edgy and nervous. But I would think the major thing was really to do with attitude. I mean none more so than Roy Aitken, the captain of the team. A lot of people have criticised him, but I tell you we wouldn't be going to Italy if it wasn't for him. Because he's been right in the middle of things there, trying to hang everything together. And when the going gets tough then he gets going. And therefore it's people like him, people like Alex McLeish, and I mean you saw Willie Miller, a really bad knee injury, Maurice Malpas, all these lads, lads with a big heart.'

On how far Scotland could go at the World Cup, Roxburgh added, 'Och well, that is for another day. I think tonight we will just go home and have a good sleep.'

Finishing second in the group probably reflected Scotland's standing: behind the impressive Yugoslavians, but ahead of the French, who struggled to find form before it was too late.

There were plenty of goals in Scotland's qualifiers, 24 all in all (12 for and 12 against). Mo Johnston was the second-top scorer in the European qualification groups, and the partnership between him and McCoist proved a vast success. They always looked like a team with goals in them, and continued creating chances in every game; even the 3-0 defeat in Paris could easily have gone the other way.

But this was also a side that was shipping goals. They conceded three times in the away games against their fiercest rivals, Yugoslavia and France, during the autumn of 1989. Against Yugoslavia, they had crumbled to concede three times within the space of six minutes, revealing a very nervous defence. The big weakness in this respect was not necessarily only the four at the back, but perhaps more significantly the midfield bank of four.

Remarkably, six of the 12 goals that Scotland conceded came from set pieces. Despite the aerial ability in the team with McLeish, Gough, Gillespie and McPherson, they often struggled to pick up their men and continued leaking goals throughout the qualification campaign.

Roxburgh stuck with a 4-4-2 formation for the entire campaign. It allowed the team to be more direct at times, and relied heavily on the work rate of the two forwards. Creativity was otherwise lacking in midfield, although McStay and Bett stood out as the two players most likely to fashion chances.

The one big issue Roxburgh had with his formation was on the left, where he struggled to find the right player. He tested several players, and eventually only Murdo MacLeod, a defensive midfielder, started more than one game in this troubled position.

Group 5 final table:

	P	W	D	L	F	A	Pts
Yugoslavia	8	6	2	0	16	6	14
Scotland	8	4	2	2	12	12	10
France	8	3	3	2	10	7	9
Norway	8	2	2	4	10	9	6
Cyprus	8	0	1	7	6	20	1

Roxburgh could savour his achievement over Christmas and the New Year. He had meticulously prepared his team throughout a long and tiring qualification campaign. In such a tough group, away form would be crucial, and that superb win in Oslo set the tone for an excellent 1988/89. The 3-2 victory in Cyprus was not pretty and, in truth, Scotland had got out of jail after a poor performance.

The key result was a rousing 2-0 win over France at Hampden in March 1989. It was the best performance of Roxburgh's reign so far and underlined once again why Johnston was among the best and most feared strikers in Europe. His six goals took Scotland to the World Cup. With only one point required from their last three games, qualification seemed like a formality by September 1989. Leading 1-0 at half-time in Yugoslavia the Scots seemed on course for Italy, before an alarming collapse led to a 3-1 defeat.

Losing in Paris was always a possibility but the 3-0 defeat flattered the French. Then, on a night of high drama, Scotland turned in a good, brave performance against Norway at Hampden in November. Only some great goalkeeping denied them a comfortable victory. Despite the late scare, the 1-1 draw was enough and the Tartan Army could pack their bags for Italy in the summer of 1990.

Roxburgh had received a huge blow when Richard Gough pulled out of the squad, injured ahead of the Norway game, so Dave McPherson filled in at right-back. Although he lacked the attacking qualities of the Rangers defender, he was good in the air and a solid player. Willie Miller, back at Hampden, looked secure enough alongside Alex McLeish, but sadly his knee injury meant that he never played for Scotland again after his 65th appearance in dark blue. The Norwegian strikers would provide the type of physical challenge that McLeish seemed to relish.

In midfield, Roxburgh sprang a surprise by playing skipper Roy Aitken wide on the right, with Jim Bett joining Paul McStay in the centre. It seemed to work quite well. He was more creative and was able to link the play between midfield and attack. McStay seemed more comfortable and was more of an attacking threat. They both kept the ball well and took the sting out of the game when it became more frantic.

Davie Cooper looked dangerous on the left, and at times linked up well with Maurice Malpas. He put in some dangerous crosses and gave the team more balance. Up front, Ally McCoist and Mo Johnston were a constant threat, with Mo so unlucky not to add to his six-goal tally. McCoist was outstanding, as his running in behind, movement and hold up play occupied the whole Norwegian back four. The striker would later claim that it was his best game for his country so far.

When Willie Miller had to come off with a knee injury, Murdo MacLeod filled in at centre-back, a calming presence alongside McLeish. The only concern of the evening was the performance of Jim Leighton in goal. Once again, he looked nervous, flapping at crosses, and his lack of confidence spread some uncertainty to the Scottish defence.

Norway's equaliser was incredible. When Erland Johnsen let fly from near the halfway line there seemed little danger, but Leighton missed the flight of the ball and was embarrassed when it went into the net. In his 2000 autobiography, *In the Firing Line*, he explained, 'It was another of those nervy occasions, even though McCoist put us in front just before the break. I was bitterly disappointed when Norway scored their equaliser in injury time, especially as Erland Johnsen's shot was hit from 40 yards. I was convinced the ball was heading past the post, when it suddenly took a tremendous bend. I've never seen anything like it before or since, for it must have moved in the air a good four yards, leaving me looking badly at fault as it went into the net. Fortunately, that freakish goal was of no consequence, but it certainly annoyed me and took the shine off my qualifying celebrations.'

Leighton had had a very mixed qualifying campaign. He was outstanding in the 2-0 win over France, but put in some nervous displays in Cyprus and Yugoslavia. He was beaten at his near post in Paris and looked vulnerable to crosses. He had kept only one clean sheet in seven qualifiers, conceding 11 goals. Andy Roxburgh had a big decision to make for the World Cup, and the pre-World Cup friendlies would give Hibs goalkeeper Andy Goram the chance to stake his claim to be first choice in Italy.

Overall, Roxburgh could be pleased with a successful qualifying campaign. A good start was vital and the narrow win in Oslo set the Scots up for a brilliant opening set of fixtures; they won four out of their first five qualifiers in 1988/89. Richard Gough's priceless two goals in Cyprus were key in a game where the Scots got out of jail. Their most impressive performance was the rousing 2-0 win over France at Hampden. Mo Johnston's brilliant overhead kick against Cyprus once again underlined his quality as a striker to be feared.

It was alarming just how badly the Scots defended in the defeats in Yugoslavia and in France. The two own goals in Zagreb were the first in three years under Roxburgh, then the return of Willie Miller to partner Alex McLeish was not a success against the talented Yugoslavs. Gough had a magnificent qualifying campaign, however; his goals, leadership and threat in the air were pivotal in getting the Scots to their fifth World Cup in a row.

Andy Roxburgh had used 27 players in qualifying. Roy Aitken, Maurice Malpas, Alex McLeish and Paul McStay had played in all eight games, while Mo Johnston had scored six goals in seven games. Steve Nicol and Ally McCoist had also impressed, and Dave McPherson and Gary Gillespie had both given Scotland a solid base at the back. Gordon Durie and Alan McInally were both useful additions in attack and Roxburgh had tried Pat Nevin, Gordon Strachan and Davie Cooper in the wide areas, with varying degrees of success.

The Scotland boss now had to find the right blend in central midfield, with Jim Bett, Murdo MacLeod and Everton's Stuart McCall different options. Gary McAllister and John Collins were two players on the fringe of the squad, hoping to stake a late claim for a place on the plane to Italy.

14

World Champions

ON 9 DECEMBER 1989 the World Cup draw took place in Rome; at that time 24 teams took part in the finals. Scotland were drawn in Group C alongside Brazil, Sweden and Costa Rica – a tough proposition on paper but with the four best third-placed teams also going through, there was every chance that Andy Roxburgh could make history and lead Scotland into the second round of a World Cup for the first time.

In preparation, he held a squad get-together in early February in Genoa, the venue for two of their group games. Several players pulled out, notably those from Rangers and Liverpool, but Roxburgh and Craig Brown found it was useful preparation for the summer. Some players like Willie Miller were injured and would not feature at the World Cup. Given that he was 35 at the time, it was doubtful that he would have been selected anyway.

Roxburgh wanted to see a few of the fringe members of his squad and blood some new players before he selected his final World Cup group. Players like Andy Goram, Bryan Gunn, Stewart McKimmie, Craig Levein, Gary Gillespie, John Collins, Gary McAllister, Stuart McCall, Murdo

MacLeod, Alan McInally, Robert Fleck and Gordon Durie would all feature in a series of friendlies leading up to the tournament.

Roxburgh had arranged matches at home to world champions Argentina, East Germany, Egypt, Poland and in Malta. The game against the Africans was strange preparation to face Costa Rica and neither Poland nor East Germany had qualified for the World Cup. The Egyptians were drawn in Group F alongside England, the Republic of Ireland and European champions the Netherlands.

29 March 1990 – Scotland 1 Argentina 0

Argentina came to Hampden for the first time since 1979. Then, a young Diego Maradona had starred in a 3-1 victory, scoring his first goal for his country. He swapped shirts with Arthur Graham after the game and was famously pictured wearing a Scotland jersey. Sadly, he was injured and did not make the trip this time. The South Americans still fielded a very strong side, featuring five of the players who had lifted the World Cup in Mexico.

Roxburgh decided to experiment with a 3-5-2 formation:

Leighton
Gough–Levein–McLeish (c)
McKimmie–McStay–Bett (Aitken 89)–McCall–MacLeod
Fleck–McInally (McClair 74)

Captain Roy Aitken, who had made a shock move from Celtic to Newcastle United, was surprisingly dropped. Would Roxburgh be prepared to play with a back three with Richard Gough in his preferred club position of centre-back at the World Cup?

There were debuts for Hearts centre-half Craig Levein, Everton midfielder Stuart McCall, and Norwich City's former Rangers striker Robert Fleck. The 51,000 crowd saw Jim Leighton in confident form, making a superb save diving at the feet of Jorge Valdano. Gough headed wide, and on 32 minutes Stewart McKimmie drove into the box to fire into the roof of the net and open the scoring. Scotland were battling well and the ball got bogged down in midfield; the visitors' physical approach led to a lot of fouls and the referee constantly stopped the game.

In the second half Claudio Caniggia began to run at the Scottish defence but Levein looked assured on his debut. Argentina forced a series of free kicks and corners, but they came to nothing. Paul McStay fired over late on and despite some late pressure Scotland secured a famous 1-0 victory to become unofficial 'world champions'.

'If you beat the world champions it has to be a great night. I don't remember much about the goal beyond thinking I had a lot of time to finish off the move,' McKimmie later told the *Daily Record*.

Murdo MacLeod recalled to the BBC Sport website in 2020, 'It turned out to be a physical game, and when we went 1-0 up, they were getting more and more involved, because they were not used to losing matches. It was a big shock for them but tremendous for us.'

Robert Fleck had made a promising debut while Alan McInally's power gave the Scots presence up front. Andy Roxburgh could be pleased with the defensive display, with Leighton back to his best in goal. It was a great result but tougher tests were still to come in Italy. The win was a huge shot in the arm for Roxburgh and his men; they had beaten the world champions and one of the giants of world football.

There was no need to get carried away but it showed that Scotland could defend well for long spells and keep their shape against opponents who dominated possession. It was a valuable test before they faced further South American giants in Brazil in Turin.

There were still areas of the team with positions up for grabs. While Leighton and Andy Goram battled over the number one jersey, there was no other natural left-back to replace Maurice Malpas. Richard Gough had an able deputy in Stewart McKimmie, but there was no obvious replacement for the Dundee United defender. At centre-back, the team looked very strong with Alex McLeish, Dave McPherson, Gary Gillespie and Craig Levein. In midfield, Stuart McCall had the chance to push for a late place in the squad. The upcoming friendlies would also give Roxburgh an opportunity to see the talented Gary McAllister and John Collins in action. Up front, Fleck, Durie and McInally all offered something different and would Roxburgh look to wingers like Cooper, Nevin and Strachan for more creativity? There were just a few more weeks left to find out.

24 April 1990 – Scotland 0 East Germany 1

In a low-key friendly, a crowd of just 21,868 saw Gary McAllister make his debut alongside John Collins, who was winning just his second cap. Gordon Durie was in attack alongside Mo Johnston. Roxburgh continued with a three-man defence of Gough, Levein and captain Alex McLeish. The East Germany team would disband at the end of the year when Germany reunified after the fall of the Berlin Wall.

McLeish headed wide from a corner and almost headed home a Collins free kick. McAllister was probing and the runs of Collins looked dangerous. Early in the second half McAllister's free kick was beaten away by Perry Bräutigam. McStay came on after 67 minutes as Scotland continued to look for the opening goal, but against the run of play the visitors took the lead. McLeish did not deal with a long goal kick and as Levein hesitated, Ulf Kirsten burst through and was pulled down by McLeish. England referee Neil Midgley pointed to the spot. Thomas Doll, later to join Celtic, sent Goram the wrong way to open the scoring. Ally McCoist had replaced Durie and he went close after a scramble in the penalty area. McAllister fired wide from inside the six-yard box late on but Scotland could find no way through and East Germany won 1-0.

For Roxburgh, there were still some positives despite the result. Goram looked calm and confident, Levein was assured, and the central midfield of McCall, McAllister and Collins looked promising. Some in the press were calling for Roy Aitken to be dropped and there was certainly a case for it, as he had looked slow and lacking confidence, though it was inconceivable that Roxburgh would leave his captain out once the World Cup started.

16 May 1990 – Scotland 1 Egypt 3

Norwich City goalkeeper Bryan Gunn made his debut at Pittodrie, his former home. Davie Cooper was a shock inclusion on the left of midfield but Roxburgh valued his skill and experience. Once again, the manager lined up with a back three of Gough, Gillespie and McLeish. Egypt were keen to test themselves against European opposition:

drawn against England, Republic of Ireland and European champions the Netherlands, they saw the game as the ideal preparation for the World Cup.

On 15 minutes Gamal Abdel-Hamid headed Egypt in front from a corner; Gunn should have done better but he could only palm the ball into the net. The visitors were a constant threat on the break, with Ahmed El-Kass running in behind the Scottish defence. On 28 minutes Durie knocked the ball back to Gunn without looking and Hossam Hassan headed the Egyptians' second goal. Gough went close with a header before McStay tested Ahmed Shobeir from long range. Durie headed narrowly wide as the Scots pressed before half-time.

Stuart McCall replaced McKimmie at the start of the second half, so Scotland reverted to a back four with Maurice Malpas moving to left-back. Cooper went close with a long-range shot and Durie fired over. Durie stabbed the ball wide before McCoist pulled a goal back, firing home a flick by Durie from the edge of the box. Durie fired wide before Ismail Youssef curled home the third on 83 minutes. Despite a series of crosses by Cooper, Gough and Bett wasted good chances and Egypt were victorious. It was a huge blow. The 3-5-2 formation did not work and Bryan Gunn had a poor game. Cooper gave some good balance on the left but the defeat left Roxburgh with more questions than answers.

19 May 1990 – Scotland 1 Poland 1

Andy Goram, who had impressed against the East Germans, regained his place in goal as Andy Roxburgh reverted to a back four of Gough, Gillespie, Levein and Malpas.

Ally McCoist almost gave Scotland the lead when he hit the post from a free kick and the rebound was scrambled clear. Goram saved well from Roman Kosecki before, on 42 minutes, Mo Johnston headed the opening goal from a cross by Ally McCoist. Scotland were ahead at the break and looking comfortable, and on the hour a long hopeful ball to the edge of the box seemed harmless but Gillespie inexplicably lobbed it neatly over Goram for an own goal.

McCoist should have given the Scots the lead soon after but he hit the bar from point-blank range. At the other end Goram did well to tip Dariusz Dziekanowski's effort around the post. A 1-1 draw was not the send-off the 25,000 crowd expected but for Roxburgh it cemented Stuart McCall's place in midfield. His energy and tackling ability gave the Scots presence in the middle, while Gary McAllister also showed that he was a more than able deputy for Paul McStay.

28 May 1990 – Malta 1 Scotland 2

In the final warm-up game before the World Cup, Andy Goram started in goal. Roxburgh brought in Dave McPherson to partner Gary Gillespie at centre-back and Jim Bett returned on the left of midfield. Alan McInally had the chance to stake his claim in attack alongside Mo Johnston.

Although it was a useful workout in front of just 3,938 fans, the game was virtually a training exercise and Roxburgh made five substitutions. Two headers by McInally gave Scotland a 2-1 victory, but they had only kept one clean sheet in their last five games. There were still questions left to answer. Who would start in goal? Would Roxburgh opt for a 3-5-2 system in Italy? Who would partner Johnston up front? Worryingly, Johnston had limped off after 68 minutes with a stomach injury, replaced by McCoist. Scotland could ill afford to be without their most potent striker at the World Cup.

15

Roxburgh Picks His Squad

WHEN ANDY ROXBURGH named his 22-man squad for the World Cup finals there were few surprises.

In goal, Jim Leighton, Andy Goram and Bryan Gunn were all solid keepers, although Gunn had performed poorly against Egypt and was clearly third choice. Goram was the player in form, performing well against East Germany and Poland. Leighton, on the other hand, was having a torrid time at Manchester United. He was famously dropped by Alex Ferguson for the 1990 FA Cup Final replay against Crystal Palace, which United won 1-0. Les Sealey offered his winners' medal to Leighton but he refused. To this day Leighton refuses to talk to Ferguson as his bitterness against his former boss remains.

Leighton was vastly experienced with 55 caps and had been outstanding in the 1986 World Cup in Mexico. However, in qualifying he had looked nervous and lacking in confidence. Never commanding in the air, he had been at fault for both goals in Cyprus and his errors led to goals for Yugoslavia and Norway. How he let a 45-yard shot by Erland Johnsen squirm through his grasp against Norway remains a mystery, although thankfully the goal came too late to matter in the end. Roxburgh was caught between loyalty to players who had played for him for years and whether to make changes and pick the men in form. He pointed out that Leighton had been outstanding against France and Argentina, and his experience would prove vital in the tournament.

In defence, Richard Gough, Alex McLeish and Maurice Malpas were all first-choice picks. Gough's ability in the air and from set pieces, not to mention his knack of scoring vital goals like the two he scored in Cyprus, made him a vital player. Roxburgh and Gough did not always see eye to eye and had a difficult relationship. Roxburgh saw him as attacking right-back, while Gough preferred to play at centre-back, his more natural position. He had formed a formidable partnership with England defender Terry Butcher at Rangers.

Malpas gave balance at left-back, was always solid and dependable, although he rarely got forward. Alex McLeish was the most experienced defender, and at the age of 31 he had played in the 1982 and 1986 World Cups. Dominant in the air, he was a very solid all-round performer. Without his injured club-mate Willie Miller alongside him, Roxburgh opted for Craig Levein of Hearts, who had impressed in the friendly games. His Tynecastle team-mate Dave McPherson was also selected. He had performed well in qualifying and both players had a good understanding from club level. McPherson could also play at right-back as well as in central defence.

Gary Gillespie was a quality defender, vastly experienced at Liverpool since 1983. Although he'd had injury problems in the past, he was capable of playing at right-back, centre-back and as a sweeper. However, he had been in poor form leading up to the World Cup, badly at fault in Yugoslavia and scored a comical own goal against Poland at Hampden.

At right-back Stewart McKimmie came in after his impressive performance and goal against Argentina. A reliable defender, he was decent going forward with good crossing ability. Steve Nicol, who had featured throughout the qualifying campaign, pulled out through injury, needing an operation at the end of the season. It was a big blow for Roxburgh as Nicol could play at right-back and left-back, as well as on both sides of midfield. Steve Clarke of Chelsea was in good form but had not featured in any of the qualifiers so was never in contention.

In midfield, Roy Aitken was the captain and an inspirational figure. However, his form had been patchy going into the World Cup. His controversial move from Celtic to Newcastle at the start of 1990 had affected his confidence and despite criticism from the press, he was always going to be one of Roxburgh's first picks. Although he was used as a defensive midfielder for Scotland, he had played most of his career as a centre-back for Celtic. Roxburgh valued his leadership as well as his strength and motivational qualities.

Paul McStay was an enigma. Talented and skilful, he was superb for Celtic, with his vision and eye for goal making him one of the best Scottish midfielders since his debut in 1983. However, he had found it hard to play consistently at international level, and despite some notable performances in qualifying, especially against France at Hampden, he had yet to convince in a Scotland shirt.

Ian Ferguson of Rangers missed out. Jim Bett of Aberdeen was an experienced player; capable of playing in central midfield or on either wing, he had a good range of passing and was dangerous from set pieces and free kicks. He was unfortunate not to play at the 1986 World Cup having been an unused substitute in Mexico.

Stuart McCall had made a late run into the team. Winning his first cap in March, he had been solid in the middle, capable of playing as a holding midfielder or on the right. His energy and tackling ability made him a valuable member of the team, and at 25 years old he had a bright future at international level.

Murdo MacLeod was playing in Germany for Borussia Dortmund. He was solid and dependable and Roxburgh's preferred choice on the left. Gary McAllister was a good option in midfield, capable of playing in the centre or either wing. John Collins was establishing himself at Hibs and his vision and skill could prove vital in Italy.

On the wing, Roxburgh had a dilemma. Although an admirer of Pat Nevin, the Chelsea player had blown hot and cold at international level. Skilful and creative, he was a right-winger, but had failed to play the position effectively. He always seemed to drift inside leaving the full-back vulnerable. He sometimes made mazy runs and went past the same defender twice before delivering the cross. He had failed to impress against England in May 1989 and had not featured since. His crossing ability was up and down and doubts about his performance and consistency meant that he missed out on the final squad.

Gordon Strachan was another player who was a contender on the right of midfield. He was enjoying a renaissance at Leeds, leading them back to the First Division at the end of the 1989/90 season. At 33 years of age he would not be able to start all of the three games, but could certainly be useful for a specific match or as a substitute. However, he had failed to impress in the 3-0 defeat in Paris and was overlooked.

Davie Cooper was enjoying a fine season at Motherwell and had made a late run to get into the squad. He had started against Norway and Egypt, but had looked subdued in both games. Now aged 34 he could provide skill and experience, with his ability to beat a man and deliver crosses. Roxburgh decided to select the winger, but unfortunately he had to pull out of the squad at the last minute. He was carrying a knock that would have prevented him from starting games, but even though he would have been fit enough to make an impact from the bench, he felt it was unfair for him to take up a place when a fit player would be available.

So Roxburgh chose Norwich striker Robert Fleck to replace him. Fleck was a consistent scorer in the First Division, and had given Glenn Hysén, the stylish Swedish centre-back and captain, a torrid time in a league game at Carrow Road, and the Liverpool defender was sent off.

In attack, Mo Johnston was the best striker available; his six goals in qualifying had taken Scotland to their fifth World Cup in a row. His controversial move from Nantes to Rangers in 1989 for £1.5m had rejuvenated his career, and it was believed that he had become the first openly Catholic player to sign for Rangers. However, it was later revealed that South African striker Don Kitchenbrand in the 1950s was the first Catholic player, but he had kept his faith hidden.

Rangers team-mate Ally McCoist was the natural choice to partner Johnston up front. He had missed a few chances against Poland, but had scored against Egypt and a vital winner against Cyprus in the qualifier at Hampden.

Gordon Durie was in good form for Chelsea and had scored in the 3-1 defeat in Yugoslavia. He was a hard-running forward, capable of playing on either wing or up front. He would go on to play for Scotland at the 1998 World Cup.

Alan McInally of Bayern Munich was the final striker selected for the squad. Although he had injury problems, he had impressed for Scotland. McInally had scored on his debut against Chile and his two goals against Malta in the final friendly before the World Cup cemented his place. Powerful in the air, he would provide the Scots with something different in attack.

Other notable strikers failed to make the squad. Graeme Sharp had not featured since 1988, and Brian McClair was in poor form for Manchester United. David Speedie had never scored for Scotland in ten games so missed out.

Charlie Nicholas would have been a surprise choice, but he had an excellent season for Aberdeen, winning the League Cup and Scottish Cup, beating both Old Firm teams in the finals. He had formed a prolific partnership with Dutch striker Hans Gillhaus, who was selected by the Netherlands in their World Cup squad. Nicholas had failed to live up to the early promise of his debut in 1983, when his brilliant lob against Switzerland at Hampden promised a bright future.

When he chose to move to Arsenal instead of Liverpool, which former Scotland manager Jock Stein had recommended, he found himself in and out of the team, mainly used as a substitute. He had played in the 1986 World Cup in Mexico but had not featured in qualifying, apart from a late substitute appearance against Cyprus.

At the time, ITV's Ian St John described it as the worst squad Scotland had ever taken to the World Cup. Looking back at the time of writing, there were some top-class players in every department. What Steve Clarke would give to have an Andy Goram, Richard Gough, Alex McLeish, Stuart McCall, Gary McAllister, John Collins and strikers of the ability of Mo Johnston and Ally McCoist.

Andy Roxburgh told *Inside Football* magazine in 1990, 'What has got Scotland to the World Cup finals is harmony. Most people in Scotland recognise that we don't have the individual geniuses we had in the past, players like Danny McGrain, Graeme Souness and Kenny Dalglish. But our present team is very much built on group effort. We try and carry the harmony in the group on to the pitch. We're about enthusiasm and organisation, and we try to highlight the skill levels available.

'We're not a team that can be left to individual brilliance, but the boys recognise that and they're very committed to team effort. We cannot depend on the helter skelter of the Premier League. If we become a kick and rush team, we're bust. The Scotland team has never been found wanting in terms of effort and commitment to the cause. Playing for Scotland is about pride, and my players will show that in June.'

Scotland 1990 World Cup squad:
Goalkeepers – 1 Jim Leighton (Manchester United), 31, 55 caps; 12 Andy Goram (Hibernian), 26, nine caps; 22 Bryan Gunn (Norwich City), 26, one cap.
Defenders – 2 Alex McLeish (Aberdeen), 31, 69 caps; 4 Richard Gough (Rangers), 28, 49 caps; 6 Maurice Malpas (Dundee United), 27, 34 caps; 11 Gary Gillespie (Liverpool),

29, 11 caps; 15 Craig Levein (Hearts), 25, five caps; 17 Stewart McKimmie (Aberdeen), 27, four caps; 19 Dave McPherson (Hearts), 26, four caps.

Midfielders – 3 Roy Aitken (Newcastle United), 31, 53 caps; 5 Paul McStay (Celtic), 25, 49 caps; 8 Jim Bett (Aberdeen), 30, 24 caps; 10 Murdo MacLeod (Borussia Dortmund), 31, 14 caps; 16 Stuart McCall (Everton), 25, five caps; 18 John Collins (Hibernian), 22, four caps; 20 Gary McAllister (Leicester City), 25, three caps.

Strikers – 7 Mo Johnston (Rangers), 27, 33 caps; 9 Ally McCoist (Rangers), 27, 23 caps; 13 Gordon Durie (Chelsea), 24, six caps; 14 Alan McInally (Bayern Munich), 27, seven caps; 21 Robert Fleck (Norwich City), 24, one cap.

16

Nightmare Opener

11 June 1990 – Scotland v Costa Rica

SCOTLAND WOULD open their campaign against the Central Americans Costa Rica in Genoa. They were managed by the Serbian Bora Milutinović and had qualified impressively, topping a group ahead of the USA, Trinidad and Tobago, Guatemala and El Salvador.

All 22 of their players were home-based and they were an unknown quantity. They had played a series of friendlies in 1990, beating the USA 2-0 in Miami before narrowly losing to Uruguay, USSR, Poland and notably Wales in Cardiff.

It was the Wales game that played a key part in Andy Roxburgh's selection for the opening group match. He had observed that the Costa Rica goalkeeper Gabelo Conejo was suspect in the air and had difficulty dealing with crosses. However, that was just a friendly and meant little in the context of the World Cup. From videos and match reports, Roxburgh was aware that Costa Rica were physically strong, skilful on the ball and played with a sweeper system. They had pacy wingers in Claudio Jara and Héctor Marchena, and striker Juan Cayasso was a good finisher.

On the morning of the game Roxburgh pointed out on ITV that Scotland were unfortunate to play Costa Rica first. He expected a tough game and they would not be underestimated. As always with Scotland, there was the worry that they would come unstuck against a so-called minnow; older supporters were still haunted by the memories of Peru and Iran from the 1978 World Cup. Although Scotland had faced Scandinavian and South American teams before, they had never come across Central American opponents. Playing Costa Rica first was a disadvantage as they would be very motivated and keen to put on a good performance in their opening game.

Bora Milutinović was a vastly experienced coach. He had managed hosts Mexico to the quarter-finals in 1986 and would later go on to manage the USA in 1994, Nigeria in 1998 and China in 2002. He had only taken over as Costa Rica manager 90 days before the start of Italia 90 and had spent the last six weeks before the tournament with players in a training camp and playing a series of friendlies behind closed doors.

Costa Rica would be well organised and a threat on the break. There was the question of whether they could respond if they went behind but they went into the World Cup with no pressure on their shoulders. The nation had a population of just three million, similar to Scotland, and the players were already regarded as heroes in their homeland just by qualifying for the World Cup. Although they would not qualify again until 2002, they followed that up in 2006 and have appeared at every World Cup since 2010. They memorably won their group in 2014, beating Uruguay 3-1, Italy 1-0 and drawing 0-0 with England. After beating Greece on penalties they reached the quarter-finals where the Netherlands beat them in a penalty shoot-out.

On Monday, 11 June, Scotland and Costa Rica lined up at the Stadio Luigi Ferraris in Genoa, the home of Sampdoria and Genoa. The Scots were in their away kit of white shirts with yellow stripes and blue shorts while Costa Rica were in red shirts and white shorts.

I remember this day vividly. I was 16 in 1990 and 11 June was the day of my final GCSE exam, in the morning. The game was shown live on ITV with commentary by Alan Parry and Billy McNeill. The major surprise in Roxburgh's team selection was him picking Alan McInally instead of Ally McCoist up front. When he announced the team in training the day before, Roxburgh said 'Mo and Nally'. McCoist misheard and it was only when Craig Brown told him it was 'Mo and big Alan' that he realised he was on the bench. With his selection it was clear that Roxburgh wanted a more direct style of football, believing that Costa Rica's weakness was in the air and their goalkeeper's inability to deal with crosses could lead to chances and goals for Scotland. Jim Leighton was chosen ahead of Andy Goram, perhaps not unexpectedly, but there was some unease among the Tartan Army that his nerves and lack of confidence could spread to the rest of the defence.

Stuart McCall later recalled to the BBC Sport website in 2022, 'There was an old story that we'd found out they had a really small goalkeeper, hence we started with big Alan McInally up front, and put in loads of high balls. But he [Conejo] was 6ft 3in and outstanding!'

Roxburgh said in the same article, 'Bora Milutinović has become a good friend of mine. He said to me, "You hadn't a clue what we would do." They played a lot of closed-door matches and practised tactics endlessly. He knew everything about us because all our warm-up matches were on public display.'

Maurice Malpas told *The Scotsman* in 2020, 'I don't think we underestimated them, it was just a case that we didn't really know too much about them. It's not like today, where you can watch as many full games as you like of any opponent you come up against. We had match reports on them and Andy Roxburgh watched them as often as possible. Looking back, getting them in the first game was not the advantage we thought it was. We didn't really know how they would set up. I know the nation expected us to beat them. The players expected us to beat them. We all felt we could take something from the game.'

Scotland assistant manager Craig Brown told *The Guardian* in 2014, 'Costa Rica were a good team then and are a good team now. You don't get to the World Cup unless you are a good side and it was arguably even harder to do that in 1990. Bora Milutinović had an excellent record with smaller nations. He took four teams [Mexico, Costa Rica, USA and Nigeria] into the second round of World Cups, which shows the coaching talent he had.'

Brown believed that inaccurate perceptions remained an issue when it came to certain international teams, 'Costa Rica isn't a traditional football nation, so people from the outside have underestimated them. But there was no question of that. You could argue that we were over-prepared for that game. The preparations were great. We had a superb training base, £100,000 had been spent on the pitch alone, just to get it ready for us. So everything was perfect before the game, the preparations had been first class.'

A crowd of 30,867 were in the stadium on a sunny afternoon and the stands were draped in Scottish flags and banners. Scotland lined up as follows:

Leighton
Gough (McKimmie HT)–McPherson–McLeish–Malpas
McCall–McStay–Aitken (c)–Bett (McCoist 73)
McInally–Johnston

Scotland started brightly; McInally got down the left and his cross was grabbed by Conejo at the second attempt. Costa Rica were neat and tidy on the ball, offloading it to each other with one or two touches. Captain Róger Flores was their sweeper, a rugged, no-nonsense defender with Mauricio Montero and Germán Chavarria alongside him. Costa Rica seemed content for Scotland to have the ball early on and looked to break quickly when they could.

With Gough, McPherson and McLeish all over six feet tall, the Scotland defence was dominant in the air, with Gough in particular a huge threat from corners and free kicks. Much would depend on the creativity of McStay and Bett in midfield, as their craft would be vital to provide service to Mo Johnston and Alan McInally. The first chance fell to Costa Rica on seven minutes, however, as Juan Cayasso fired wide from the edge of the box.

Just two minutes later a foul on McStay gave Scotland a free kick 25 yards out. After a long run-up, Bett blasted the ball against the wall and it was cleared. Costa Rica were keeping the ball well, Jara was running at Malpas and Montero was beating McInally in the air. Cayasso was finding space on the edge of the Scotland penalty area and was linking up the attack well.

The Costa Ricans were marking the Scots man for man, and it was captain Roy Aitken who almost broke the deadlock. He ran from deep and fired a long-range shot just wide, with Conejo scrambling. McInally then found space on the edge of the area but his touch let him down and the ball was scrambled clear.

On 25 minutes McStay's free kick on the right was met by Gough in the six-yard box but his header flew over the bar. Scotland also forced a series of corners that came to nothing. McCall linked up well with Johnston, and laid the ball off to the Everton midfielder who fired wide from the edge of the box.

On 40 minutes Gough headed the ball back to Johnston who smashed it from the edge of the six-yard box, but Conejo made a flying save to push it away for a corner. At the other end, Cayasso's free kick was cleared as Scotland tried to quicken the tempo towards half-time. Scotland lacked width with Gough and Malpas not getting forward enough from full-back. Bett looked out of sorts and McCall was battling well but without much support. McStay had looked like the man most likely to create something for the Scots but at half-time it was still 0-0.

Gough did not appear for the second half and was replaced by Stewart McKimmie. The Rangers man flew home after the game for an operation on a toe injury.

Maurice Malpas explained to the *Courier Evening Telegraph*, 'It was the first time Costa Rica qualified for the World Cup and they were an unknown quantity, whereas we were regular qualifiers back then. We were big favourites and pressure came with that. What we quickly discovered was that they were very good technically and could put in a nasty tackle or two. We had a settled defence at the time but all that changed when Richard Gough suffered an injury and did not come out for the second half. It was unsettling and we definitely missed him, particularly his goal threat in the air and set pieces.'

Gough had made his 50th appearance for Scotland. He later told Archie Macpherson in *Adventures in the Golden Age – Scotland in the World Cup Finals 1974–1998*, 'I had this chronic toe injury which I was getting injections for to keep playing. It had been going on for some time. As soon as I knew that I couldn't fight on and the pain was so intense I had to give up. As for leaving the camp after the Costa Rica game that was organised by Graeme Souness, who flew me directly to Harley Street for essential treatment. Nothing other than that.'

On 50 minutes Costa Rica took the lead following a flowing move which found Jara on the edge of the area. He back-heeled the ball to Cayasso who lifted it over the onrushing Leighton. It was a huge blow and made Scotland's task even harder. The Costa Ricans now had something to hold on to, and could hit the Scots on the break. A goal behind, fans watching at home and on the terraces knew the team needed to score at least twice to get a win. With hindsight, a 1-1 draw would have been a decent result, though it would have been seen as a disaster at the time. The goal revived memories of Peru and Iran in 1978 and New Zealand in 1982 as once again Scotland had conceded to weaker opposition. Some players and supporters felt Costa Rica had no right to beat them, but Scotland were finding out to their cost once again that there are no easy games at international level.

Maurice Malpas told the *Courier Evening Telegraph*, 'The manager wanted all our play to go through the middle of the park. At United I was used to getting up and down the line, but we were told by Andy to push everything inside where we had big Roy Aitken and Stuart McCall. At their goal I showed their player inside as instructed but on this occasion Roy wasn't there and we paid the price when they scored.'

Scotland tried to hit back and straight away they forced two corners but Dave McPherson headed one wide and Conejo claimed the other confidently. That feeling of doom and impending disaster, familiar to all Scotland supporters, was beginning to come to the surface. As I watched on TV I felt that there was still plenty of time for Scotland to come back, but I wanted Ally McCoist to come on as soon as possible.

As the game drifted on, Scotland looked laboured in midfield. A free kick on the edge of the box was a good chance to draw level, but Jim Bett blasted the ball miles over the bar. At the other end Jara turned sharply but fired wide of the far post. Alan McInally had a clear header but headed over from McCall's cross, McStay hooked the ball over, and then came the best chance of the match. McKimmie crossed, Johnston turned in the six-yard box but Conejo spread himself to block the shot, and McStay's follow-up was cleared off the line. Was it going to be one of those days for Scotland?

Jara got free on the edge of the box in search of Costa Rica's second goal but his tame effort was gathered by Leighton. Roy Aitken then struck the ball cleanly but wide, before McCoist replaced Jim Bett on 74 minutes. The Rangers striker headed straight at Conejo, and Scotland missed another good chance when McPherson sliced a free kick well wide from the edge of the box. They were looking more and more desperate.

From a corner Johnston almost turned the ball home but his effort was scrambled off the line. McPherson had gone forward to support Johnston and McCoist. Once again, McStay had failed to have an impact in a Scotland shirt, while Bett had been poor. Aitken looked laboured and the Scots lacked the imagination to break down the Costa Rica defence.

Rónald González curled a shot wide and Leighton was relieved to see the ball miss the target as he dived full length. In injury time McCoist fired over with an overhead kick but that was the last attempt and Costa Rica secured a famous victory.

I think it was without doubt the most humiliating result in Scotland history. A stunned Andy Roxburgh pointed to the amount of possession and corners Scotland had, and that they had been caught on the break by a sucker punch. He told the BBC post-match, 'The players and the backroom staff and so on and the officials who have put everything into it, they equally feel terribly bad for all the supporters. Who put so much into it as well by coming away out here. And this was one of those games that sometimes happen in football, where in the cup competition the smaller team beats the so-called bigger team. And the breakaway goal, and their goalkeeper having a daft day and we just couldn't put the ball in the net.'

Roxburgh reflected to BBC Sport in 2022, 'We could have won 3-1 or 4-1. Maurice Johnston had a couple of chances that normally would have ended up in the back of the net.'

Craig Brown told *The Guardian* in 2014, 'It wasn't like we were outplayed in the game at all. Mo Johnston should have scored a couple. If you look back at the game in isolation, we were unlucky, albeit you couldn't really say that at the time.'

The front-page headline in the *Daily Record* the next day was 'Stop The World I Want To Get Off', while the *Glasgow Evening Times*'s back page read 'Show Us The Way Home'.

Mo Johnston said in *Adventures in the Golden Age*, 'Look, let's get it right, we should have won that game. Easy to say now of course. So I blame myself. I should have scored at least a couple of goals.'

Stuart McCall recalled to the *Liverpool Echo* in 2022, 'We got beat 1-0 and as we were trudging off down the tunnel, fans were throwing their scarves at us, telling us we were a disgrace. I remember ringing my mum and dad and the family back home, and I just felt hugely embarrassed and disappointed.'

For two members of the Tartan Army who had planned their trip at the last minute, the game was a total disaster. Alison Durie and her boyfriend Paul Kirk were both students at the University of Glasgow and had travelled to Genoa without tickets. Paul explained, 'We had finished our exams and decided to fly to Italy on the spur of the moment. Some other people we knew were going so we thought we would go there and soak up the atmosphere. There was no accommodation available so the police used to let us sleep in the railway station overnight, before they would chase us out with our sleeping bags about 6am.

'We were surprised McInally started ahead of McCoist and when I saw we were in that awful away kit, I had a bad feeling it would be a long afternoon.

'At full time we booed the team off. Roxburgh looked crushed as he left the pitch. The players were too ashamed to look at us or clap us, they just ran off the park.

'We couldn't even drown our sorrows as there was a 24-hour alcohol ban on the day of every game. We bumped into some Sweden fans and they were a good laugh. They lost 2-1 to Brazil so it was do or die in the next game against us.'

Alison recalled, 'We heard that you could get some tickets from a couple of bars and cafes on the morning of the game and we managed to get two tickets for the Costa Rica game behind the goal. We didn't know what to expect from them but before the game everything seemed good. The weather was great, a great stadium and the local Italians were friendly.

'The fans underestimated Costa Rica, no question. We thought we would beat them by a couple of goals no problem. When they scored it was their first shot on target. The longer the game went on, the more we didn't look like we could score. Mo missed some great chances.

'Looking back now, it was typical Scotland. We beat world champions Argentina a few months before and then lose to Costa Rica. It was so humiliating. We didn't even know where Costa Rica was on a map, then they turned us over.

'I was upset and wanted to go home, but we decided to stay a few days longer. We decided not to go to any more Scotland games, we expected Sweden and Brazil to beat us.'

Lifelong friends and Tartan Army foot soldiers Tam Ferguson, Ian Black and Archie Greig had been following Scotland for over ten years home and away. They got tickets for all three games through the Scotland travel club. There were between 10,000 and 20,000 Scotland supporters in Italy that summer.

Tam recalled, 'We flew in from Glasgow on 10 June, the day before the game. We managed to find a campsite about two hours outside Genoa, so it was just our sleeping bags and get on with it.

'I always felt Roxburgh was too cautious. It seemed like he always went out not to lose the game and then try and nick something through Johnston or Gough on a set piece. I remember shouting at McStay who used to drive me mad. He was outstanding for Celtic but seemed to shrink when he put on a Scotland shirt.'

Archie added, 'We expected to beat Costa Rica, draw with Sweden and lose to Brazil. It seemed a good fixture to start with against Costa Rica. The local Italians in the crowd started to cheer for them when they scored and we got more and more frustrated.

'You want to say it was a shock but it was typical Scotland. Costa Rica looked like a good side and they proved it in their next two games.'

Ian said, 'I remember that Bett and McStay were shocking in that game. Aitken looked old and tired. McCoist should have started. We played too many long balls and McInally did nothing.

'At full time we couldn't get out of the ground fast enough. I'm just glad we didn't bump into any England or Ireland fans, who would have wound us up like hell.'

Beaten by no-hopers Costa Rica, how on earth could Scotland now get results against Sweden or Brazil? As he reflected on the defeat in his hotel room in Rapello, the squad's base for the tournament, Andy Roxburgh knew Scotland had been unlucky, but that was no consolation. Next up were dark horses Sweden, who topped England's group to qualify for the finals. Going into the World Cup, they hadn't lost a competitive game since a 2-1 defeat against Italy in Naples in 1987.

Craig Brown told the *Shoot the Breeze podcast* in 2020, 'Andy was an extremely serious man. He was meticulous in everything he turned his hand to. Nothing was left undone and he could go into incredible detail to organise and prepare for games. In a football context, especially with a match looming, Andy didn't appreciate much humour. I could face up to some adversities with a joke or quip, to lighten the situation. Andy didn't have a sense of humour. It would have helped him if he had, so in fact I was good for him. I could see the other side of things that weren't as dark and in the dressing room put in some banter which helped.'

It was obvious that changes had to be made. Jim Bett and Paul McStay were poor, and Bett would never play for Scotland again. Roxburgh had struggled for four years to get the best out of McStay. He looked tired after a long, hard season which only concluded in mid-May with a defeat to Aberdeen on penalties in the Scottish Cup Final. Why could he not produce consistently in a Scotland shirt? Maybe it was his mentality, as he seemed to lack confidence when wearing dark blue. With Sweden next, the Scotland midfield needed to be very solid and full of running. Could Gary McAllister provide the creative spark in the middle? John Collins was also more than capable.

In attack, Alan McInally had failed against Costa Rica. His touch was poor and he lost more headers than he won. He missed a great chance in the second half, a free header in the six-yard box, and never played for Scotland again. His record of three goals in eight games was very good on paper, but he was not the answer against the Swedes.

Would Ally McCoist start against Sweden? It seemed obvious that Robert Fleck would be in the team. His performance for Norwich City against Liverpool's Glenn

Hysén in the English First Division game, where he ran him ragged and got him sent off, gave him the nod up front. Could Gordon Durie come in as well on the wing? Would Roy Aitken stay in front of the back four or move to the right?

I think it would have been harsh to drop Jim Leighton, who did not have a save to make against Costa Rica. In defence, Roxburgh had a dilemma. Stewart McKimmie, Gary Gillespie and Dave McPherson had all played at right-back before. Would Craig Levein come in or would Roxburgh save him to face the Brazilians?

Roxburgh recalled on the STV programme *Faith, Hope and Calamity* in 1994, 'That was probably the best week's work I ever had in my life after Costa Rica. When I look back on it now, because it was a crisis, it was a crisis for everybody. I remember the banner headlines on the newspaper front page, not back page, "Stop The World I Want To Get Off". I had to work flat out that week to bring morale back up, to get the team organised and so on. We were playing Sweden and we had to win it, even if it meant we were still knocked out of the championship.'

17

Scotland's Swedish Sensation

16 June 1990 – Scotland v Sweden

SWEDEN WERE very beatable despite their impressive recent record. They had not played at a World Cup since 1978, but had an experienced team. Several of their players were playing in Italy, Portugal and at Dutch giants Ajax. Right-back Roland Nilsson, at the time of Sheffield Wednesday, and captain Glenn Hysén of Liverpool were used to the physicality and pace of the British game. They had played well against Brazil and were unfortunate not to earn a point.

After losing to Costa Rica, in some ways the pressure was off Scotland, and to many critics they were already out of the World Cup. They were clear underdogs to beat Sweden and that suited them.

Sweden had qualified impressively. Drawn in Group 2 alongside England, Poland and Albania, they went unbeaten. They began with a 0-0 draw at Wembley, with a defensive masterclass by Hysén.

Wins over Poland and Albania home and away and another goalless draw at home to England saw them win the four-team group, with England also qualifying as one of the best second-placed teams.

	P	W	D	L	F	A	Pts
Sweden	6	4	2	0	9	3	10
England	6	3	3	0	10	0	9
Poland	6	2	1	3	4	8	5
Albania	6	0	0	6	3	15	0

Coached since 1986 by Olle Nordin, Sweden were expected to reach the second round, and even the quarter-finals or beyond. Baby-faced young striker Tomas Brolin was their new star and he would be snapped up by Parma after the World Cup for £1.2m. He would later star at Euro 92, scoring a famous winning goal in a 2-1 victory over England. He was then a key part of the Sweden side that finished third at the 1994 World Cup in the USA.

10 June 1990 – Brazil 2 Sweden 1

When the sides met in Turin in the new Stadio Delle Alpi, a crowd of 62,628 turned up to catch a glimpse of 1989 Copa América winners Brazil. They were one of the favourites but were not as skilful as the 1982 side and adopted a more defensive 3-5-2 European style. Brazil were very unlucky in 1986 in Mexico, conceding just one goal in five games but going out in the quarter-finals to European champions France on penalties after an epic encounter.

Brazil were managed by 40-year-old Sebastião Lazaroni. They had top strikers like Careca and Romário, and the rest of the squad were big and strong, but the team lacked creativity and width. In Cláudio Taffarel, they had arguably Brazil's greatest ever goalkeeper. Future captain Dunga was also a key player but doubts remained over whether Brazil could finally win the World Cup again for the first time in 20 years.

Brazil kicked off in their traditional yellow shirts and blue shorts with Sweden in their away strip of all blue. Müller broke through on the right but fired wide as Brazil took control early on. Brolin tested Taffarel who got down well to save, then Branco fired wide from long range, before, on 40 minutes, Brazil took the lead as Careca beat the offside trap and rounded Ravelli to score. Brazil continued to attack in the second half but only a diving save at the feet of Brolin by Taffarel denied Sweden an equaliser; then on 63 minutes Müller crossed for the unmarked Careca to score again. Stefan Pettersson fired a long-distance drive that Taffarel saved and Branco was denied by Ravelli. Then in the 79th minute Sweden pulled a goal back when Brolin turned well at the edge of the box and fired home. Late on, Alemão was denied by Ravelli, and Careca headed over from close range. Pettersson sliced a free kick wide before Careca headed over, and in the last few minutes Jonas Thern curled a shot just over the bar. Brazil won 2-1 but Sweden had shown that they were a very capable side and that they had a strong attacking threat.

16 June 1990 – Scotland v Sweden

It has to be said that since 1974 Scotland have had some very tough World Cup draws: world champions Brazil and Yugoslavia in 1974; the Netherlands and Copa América holders Peru in 1978; Brazil again in 1982, one of their greatest ever teams and USSR. Also, the Group of Death in 1986: West Germany, Denmark and South American champions Uruguay. Then Brazil again in 1990, but, with third-placed teams also making the second round, Scotland still had a chance. A win and a draw would be enough to go through, but even just one win in three games could still let you scrape through, depending on other results.

Much of the build-up before the Sweden game focussed on the players having a night out after the Costa Rica defeat. The press had pictures of Mo Johnston and Jim Bett with glasses of champagne in hand, posing for pictures with local girls. Andy Roxburgh had given the players permission to have a meal and a few drinks together in town, and they all returned to the hotel way before midnight.

The *Daily Record* headline in the sports pages after the Costa Rica defeat read 'Worst In The World', and Alex Cameron wrote, 'They were a disgrace.' However, by the eve of the Sweden game he had written more reflectively, 'There is no question they had dreadful luck at times.'

The *Glasgow Herald* did not think Scotland had a chance after losing to Costa Rica. Under the headline 'Our Task A Mission Impossible', James Traynor wrote, 'In various parts of the city, groups of bedraggled figures trudged the streets. Their gaudy tartans, which had been perceived before the early kick-off in the Stadio Luigi Ferraris as celebrations of Scottish confidence and optimism, looked garish and someone's idea of a cruel joke in the aftermath of our defeat.'

A *Glasgow Herald* editorial before the Sweden game read, 'Oh well. Oh dear. Once again, the Scottish football team has dumped the nation into depression. You cannot really blame the players. They tried their best. They were unlucky.'

They had been unlucky. The result was awful, yet another Scotland hard-luck story. Was it the worst performance from a Scotland team in the World Cup? A 1-1 draw with Iran in 1978 and a 0-0 draw in 1986 against the ten men of Uruguay were far worse.

On the morning of the Sweden game, Roxburgh told the BBC, 'We had a blow against Costa Rica, but that's gone now. We can't do anything about it. Against Sweden, we've got a chance to put things right, to give our supporters something to cheer. You will see a very different Scotland performance tonight. Sweden have to win too, and it will be like a British-style cup tie.'

The players were determined to bounce back and beat Sweden. Maurice Malpas told *The Guardian* in 2020, 'There was a fair bit of flak flying around after the Costa Rica game and that lasted up until the next game against Sweden. But that's how the cookie crumbles. The day after the Costa Rica game we had some free time and a few of us went into the village for a bit of lunch. It soon became clear just how angry the Scotland supporters were; they really didn't like us or want to see us.

'The Scottish fans are not normally like that, they usually managed to find the positive side of things in my experience. But the guys we encountered that day couldn't see the positive side of anything! Everyone felt it was a certain victory against Costa Rica. We felt we had a real chance to start with a win but, let's be honest, we just weren't good enough on the day.'

Captain Roy Aitken told STV on the day of meeting the Scandinavians, 'The boys are desperate to put the defeat behind us. We know how shocked and upset everybody was, but we felt the performance was OK, we just didn't get the breaks. Sweden will be favourites, but being underdogs suits us. It is do or die tonight, and we are up for the battle.'

On the way to the ground, Roxburgh saw a huge banner that read, 'Don't worry Andy your P45 is in the post.' To emphasise that he was a Scotland supporter as well as manager, Roxburgh wore a tartan scarf on the bench. Craig Brown noticed a determination in training and a belief that the team were ready to battle the Swedes and get a result, even if it was only a point.

Brown and Roxburgh thought long and hard about what line-up should face the Swedes. They had carefully studied their match against Brazil, and both of the qualifying fixtures against England on video. They decided to bring Craig Levein into the side, as his pace would be able to deal with the quick Swedish forwards. Dave McPherson moved to right-back. In midfield, out went McStay and Bett and in came Murdo MacLeod and Gordon Durie. In a surprise move, Roy Aitken was moved to the right of midfield, with Durie on the left rather than MacLeod, who usually played there. McCall and MacLeod provided bite and energy in the centre and Durie was asked to supplement the strikers. Robert Fleck replaced McInally up front. His pace and movement would cause problems to the Swedish defence and Glenn Hysén in particular. Mo Johnston, heavily criticised for misses against Costa Rica, retained his place.

Sweden fielded ten players who played abroad. Most of their players were in their early 20s and their line-up contained some famous names, including captain Glenn Hysén, Jonas Thern who would later join Rangers, and Anders Limpar who joined Arsenal after the tournament and won the league title in 1990/91. Also in were Sheffield Wednesday full-back Roland Nilsson and striker Stefan Pettersson, who had scored for Gothenburg in their defeat of Dundee United in the 1987 UEFA Cup Final.

Manager Olle Nordin told the BBC, 'I could not believe the Costa Rica result. Some of our players did not see the game and thought we were joking when they heard the result. This is not to be taken as any sign of weakness by us. I know what Scotland can be like.'

Famously, Scotland seemed to psyche out their opponents in the tunnel before the game. Craig Levein recalled in *The Scotsman* in 2020, 'Even before we went out on to the field, the dressing room was hyper. People were banging their heads off doors, thumping their chests and all that sort of stuff. It was so intense. Everybody was shouting and I think that did have an impact on Sweden. The determination even in training that week had been obvious and before we went out to start the match the focus and determination was enormous.

'Normally in a dressing room there will be two or three people who will be doing most of the shouting and encouraging and cajoling, making sure everyone is up for it already. But in that dressing room I think everybody was at it. There were a lot of strong characters. Big Alex McLeish was there, Maurice Malpas, Roy Aitken was like a warrior. Big Slim [Dave McPherson] is quite a quiet but very determined guy and the list goes on. Stuart McCall is a strong character as well, a hardy player. There were a lot of good players and good characters and we were raring to go. We were determined to make up for the Costa Rica match.'

Stuart McCall recalled in the *Liverpool Echo* in 2022, 'I played in nearly 1,000 games in my career and there were probably only one or two that I could point to and say they were won in the tunnel and that was one of them. It was *Braveheart* on steroids. Roy Aitken was roaring. We had big Alex McLeish with his shot of ginger hair and freckles. Jim

Leighton without his teeth and Robert Fleck didn't have his falsers either, half our team didn't. You looked across at the opposition and even though they were Scandinavian, they were all bronzed adonises and immaculate, and we looked like a bunch of lads you'd just pulled out of the local estate. Because we'd let the country down so badly in the previous game, it was all or nothing for us.'

Maurice Malpas told *The Scotsman* in 2020, 'The Sweden game was a typical response from Scotland. We had our backs to the wall, nothing to lose and everything to gain. So we went out and did it. I think people might have preferred it the other way round. If we'd beaten Costa Rica, they could have accepted it if we'd lost to Sweden. But that's the Scottish mentality, let's do things the wrong way round.'

The game was shown live in Scotland but in the rest of the UK, England v the Netherlands was shown instead. The European champions against the team they beat 3-1 at Euro 88 was taking place at the same time as Scotland v Sweden. It would finish goalless.

Although Sweden were unbeaten in qualifying for Italy ahead of England, they were suspect in the full-back positions. Despite beating Brazil 2-1 in a friendly, in the summer of 1989 they were hammered 6-0 by Denmark and 4-2 by France. They had also lost a friendly 2-1 in the UAE in February 1990. Glenn Hysén told *Inside Football* magazine in 1990, 'We won't underestimate Scotland but if it does come down to us or them, then I'm confident we'll qualify.'

Roy Aitken made one final rallying cry before the game, in the *Daily Record*, 'We've got to be positive and go for the win. It might be the first end-to-end match of the tournament. We are sure we're better than them, now we have to prove it.'

Andy Roxburgh also told the *Daily Record*, 'When you bleed, we bleed. The players are punters themselves. If they weren't playing, they'd be there on the terraces.'

Sweden were without the injured prolific Benfica striker Mats Magnusson, but surprisingly there was no place for Glenn Strömberg or the experienced Johnny Ekström.

Leighton

McPherson–Levein–McCleish–Malpas

Aitken (c)–McCall–MacLeod–Durie (McStay 75)

Fleck (McCoist 84)–Johnston

Sweden kicked off in yellow shirts and blue shorts with Scotland back in their traditional colours of blue shirts and white shorts. After a few heavy tackles in midfield, Sweden forced the first opening on three minutes as midfielder Joakim Nilsson got free down the left and cut the ball back to left-back Stefan Schwarz, who fired over. It was an early warning for Scotland about Sweden's speed and quick thinking. The Scots looked up for the midfield battle, however, and Durie combined well with Malpas on the left but his cross was scrambled clear.

The Swedes looked very confident on the ball, spreading their passes from midfield and finding their men. On ten minutes Durie played a long crossfield pass to Fleck who forced a corner. Murdo MacLeod's delivery was flicked on by McPherson and Stuart McCall stabbed the ball home at the far post to make it 1-0 to Scotland. He told the *Liverpool Echo* in 2022, 'I was supposed to be on the edge of the six-yard box and that was me not doing what I was told as usual. We'd worked on corner routines and had big Davy McPherson on the near post who was about 6ft 4in and just nicked it on and I arrived late. I was always deadly from a yard, I could never miss. I think I just pipped Mo Johnston to it and took it off his boot. Fortunately, I got my one and only goal for Scotland in 40 internationals. I always say when you've scored in the World Cup you don't want to blot your copybook and grab goals in meaningless qualifiers. That's my excuse and I'm sticking to it!'

Disbelief registered among the Scotland supporters; a side that had been unable to beat Costa Rica had taken only 11 minutes to penetrate one of Europe's top defences. The Scotland defence was holding firm, despite the fact that the back four had never played together before. Robert Fleck, who had been in a bar in Yugoslavia when he found out he was in the squad, crossed well from the left and Ravelli grabbed the ball off Johnston's head.

Sweden responded and Peter Larsson found space on the edge of the box but fired well wide. They were fortunate to win a free kick when Levein was harshly judged to have fouled, but Leighton held Thern's effort comfortably. Aitken's long throw was flicked on by McCall but nobody followed up at the back post at the other end. Scotland were very compact and Malpas was getting forward well on the left, with Aitken staying in position on the right.

Thern volleyed wide from the edge of the area for Sweden, but Scotland were mixing their game up, playing long balls up to Johnston and Fleck but overlapping on the left with Malpas and Durie. McCall and MacLeod already looked far better than McStay and Bett did against Costa Rica. They were snapping into their tackles and not allowing the Swedes any time on the ball.

Glenn Hysén bundled over Fleck on the edge of the area as he threatened to run through on goal, and from the free kick MacLeod's effort was held by Ravelli. On 32 minutes Limpar drove a free kick well wide from 30 yards; then Thern then wasted another free kick when he curled an effort wide from 25 yards. A few minutes later Aitken went down the right, beat his man and fired in a dangerous cross. Johnston just missed the ball and Malpas headed wide.

So far, Brolin had not been in the game at all, well marshalled by the superb Levein and McLeish. However, he almost got free just before half-time, but he fouled McLeish before hitting the post, although the whistle had already been blown. At half-time Scotland led 1-0.

At the start of the second half Sweden enjoyed a spell of possession. They started to knock more long balls, and the wisdom of the decision by Roxburgh to play McPherson at right-back became evident. At the other end Fleck pounced on a mistake by the Swedish defence but shot wide with Ravelli stranded. He then fired behind after a long throw, and Aitken found space on the right, but his cross was scrambled clear.

On 54 minutes Brolin almost scored the equaliser after he danced past Aitken but Leighton saved well at his near post. Thern then lunged into McPherson and was booked, before the Swedes upped the tempo and forced a series of corners. Johnny Ekström, the tall, blond striker, replaced Stefan Pettersson on 62 minutes. He had scored the winner against England in a 1-0 friendly victory in 1986 and his pace would provide another test for the Scotland defence.

Alex McLeish was dominant and did well to head the ball back to Leighton after Brolin had threatened to run through. Scotland were allowing the Swedes to play the ball around at the back and were pressing well in midfield. Johnston was winning more and more headers and Ravelli had to race off his line to head clear from the

Rangers striker midway through the second half. Atalanta midfielder Glenn Strömberg replaced centre-back Peter Larsson on 75 minutes, as the Swedes pressed desperately for an equaliser.

Andy Roxburgh then took off Durie for Paul McStay on 76 minutes as the Tartan Army continued to roar the Scots on from the stands, with 'Flower of Scotland' ringing out as the game entered its final stages. Fleck then found space on the left, knocked the ball to McStay, who found Johnston, but his touch was heavy and the Swedish defence cleared. On 79 minutes McCall released Johnston, who ran through but Ravelli blocked his shot with his legs.

A minute later McLeish played a diagonal pass to Fleck, who found Aitken bursting through the midfield. Ravelli parried his shot and Roland Nilsson brought him down before he could fire in the rebound. Paraguayan referee Carlos Maciel pointed to the spot and Johnston confidently swept the penalty home to give Scotland a priceless 2-0 lead with his 14th goal in 35 internationals.

He said in *Adventures in the Golden Age*, 'Actually I wasn't the penalty taker, it was either big Roy or Coisty if he had been on. I took it because I wanted it more than anybody. I just grabbed the ball. Of course I knew that if I was to miss it might haunt me for the rest of my life. Then I began to think, I'm just 12 yards out, what better chance can you have to score? Then it was just another penalty. So I put it the opposite way the keeper was moving, that was all.'

On 84 minutes Ally McCoist replaced Fleck, who had run himself into the ground, but one minute later Sweden pulled a goal back. A hopeful long pass by Nilsson saw the Scots defence hesitate and Strömberg reacted quickest to guide the ball home from inside the six-yard box. Leighton could have come for it but he left it to his defenders who were caught flat-footed.

Sweden sensed blood and began to pump long balls into their front men. They were awarded a free kick on the edge of the area despite McPherson winning a clean header but justice was done when Schwartz drove the ball well wide. In injury time Leighton saved at point-blank range from Ekström, who was flagged offside anyway, and the final whistle blew soon afterwards.

The Scottish lion roared and a display full of pride, passion, battling qualities and some skill meant Scotland were still in the World Cup having almost certainly knocked Sweden out. As the players swapped shirts and applauded the Tartan Army, Roxburgh waved his tartan scarf in a show of relief and emotion. The manager had got his tactics spot on and his team selections were inspired.

Craig Levein told *The Scotsman* in 2020, 'It was quite a tense game and there was obviously quite a bit to play for. We knew that if we didn't win that game because we were playing Brazil in the next match, then the chances of getting through were slim. So the pressure was on. I think it was handled really well by the guys, especially those who started the match. We didn't lose our focus and it was a really determined display from everybody, thankfully that was good enough.

'A lot of the Scotland matches I played in we were under a lot of pressure and you felt it was backs to the wall. But that night we had a good side and when they scored late on I just felt annoyed. For me, that goal tarnished it a little bit, because we had been fairly comfortable and for long spells in the match they got nothing from us.'

Maurice Malpas told the *Courier Evening Telegraph* in 2020, 'After the stick we got for the Costa Rica defeat, we were determined to get it right next time. You don't need to be Einstein to realise that we needed to beat Sweden to have any chance of keeping our hopes alive going into the Brazil match.

'It was without doubt the best we played [in the World Cup] and we were comfortable in the game. It was a nice relief to have gotten the fans back onside. Sweden scored late on but that made the scoreline flatter them a bit. We were happy and positive after the final whistle, and were really looking forward to carrying the momentum into the Brazil match.'

Andy Roxburgh told the BBC post-match, 'Well, obviously it was an emotional night. It is very important in the management side of things you try to contain that, and you don't go overboard. But I must admit when the ball went in the net twice, you react. It was the kind of game we predicted to our own players, and there was nothing different from what they expected to find. And of course it was very much a midfield battle, because it was like a British cup tie and I'm sure everybody enjoyed it.'

Tam, Archie and Ian had a night they would never forget.

Tam said, 'We had a long day building up to the game. We were determined to enjoy ourselves, no matter what the result.

'When we got to the ground we saw a mass of Scottish flags and lion rampants. There were Swedish fans at both ends of the ground too, all mixing well together.

'When we scored first, the whole weight lifted and Costa Rica was forgotten. We were playing some good stuff and the midfield looked strong. McCall and MacLeod were pressing and biting into tackles. Even big Roy Aitken looked better on the right.

'We celebrated long into the night, but still no beers with a 24-hour alcohol ban. The Swedes were still in good voice despite the defeat. The atmosphere was great. The local Italians were great too, congratulating us and tooting their car horns as we walked past.

'It was typical Scotland; we lose to rank outsiders Costa Rica then beat one of the best teams in Europe a few days later!'

Ian said, 'There was a marching band in the afternoon and lads with tartan scarves and kilts marched through the local square with Swedish fans. It was all good-natured.

'When we saw the team we fancied our chances. I knew Fleck would cause them problems and Levein was a class defender.

'We never felt that one goal would be enough and, for me, Jim Leighton looked nervous but he played well and he celebrated at the end.

'We looked like a completely different team, full of pride and passion. The boys did Scotland proud.

'Mexico 1986 was a good trip, great weather, but on the park a disaster. Just one goal in three games and only one point. This was different, I loved it.'

Archie added, 'The Swedish fans were great, they were really up for the game and told us what they were going to do to us!

'We saw Roxburgh walking to the bench with his tartan scarf. The players looked determined and you could sense that they were up for the battle.

'We brought on McStay and McCoist which showed just how strong our squad was. When we got the penalty we didn't know who would take it. When wee Mo smashed it home we knew that we had won the game. It was magic!

'We hadn't seen a win at a World Cup since 1982 when we beat New Zealand 5-2. It was so long ago. The relief was incredible.'

Moira Black and her husband Jim had returned to Italy for the first time since their honeymoon in 1987. Moira explained, 'I was a teacher then and had somehow managed to get some time off. At my school the exams had finished by 7 June, so we thought why not go for it?

'On the morning of the Sweden game, the guy who ran the local restaurant, Giuseppe, told us that a few tickets were still available. So he sent us off to the local travel centre or tourist information office. It was about noon and we got two tickets for £60; quite dear but worth it. Once other fans heard that tickets were still available the queues started to build.

'I didn't fancy us to be honest. I couldn't see us getting more than a point or a draw but with Scotland you never know what you're going to get!

'We wanted Italy to win the World Cup but they were so unlucky. For me, it was the best World Cup Scotland have ever had. We had qualified five times in a row and just expected to be at the World Cup. Little did we know that we'd only qualify for one more World Cup since.'

Jim reflected, 'We had a lovely time in Genoa after the wedding and so decided to return to Italy for a lovely holiday. We travelled without tickets. We enjoy sightseeing, going to museums and old buildings and old churches, so we knew we would have a great time. After we lost to Costa Rica we had tried to forget about the football to be honest!

'I said it was a once-in-a-lifetime chance. When else would we be able to see Scotland play in a World Cup in

Europe? We are both Hearts fans so we were delighted to see Levein and McPherson start.

'It was very intense. Once we scored early the nerves began to settle and we never looked like surrendering our advantage.

'We flew back on the Monday but had a great week in Italy. As the time goes on, the memories still come back, it was very special.'

Jim said that Moira felt she had a hand in the victory, 'Moira claimed that we only won because she threw a coin into the town fountain and made a wish!'

Moira added, 'It was me! But seriously, it was a magical night, great memories.'

* * *

I was 16 in 1990. The Sweden game was the first time I had seen Scotland win a World Cup finals match. I had somehow missed watching the 5-2 win over New Zealand as a kid when I lived in Glasgow. It was an incredible feeling. We were the only British side to win a game so far, as England and the Republic of Ireland had drawn both of their games. I got the *Sunday Mail* which had a colour special on the match. Those few days before playing Brazil were magic, I could totally relax and enjoy the other World Cup games.

As time has gone on, the Italia 90 World Cup legend seems to have grown. It was a glorious, long, hot summer in the UK. Football was changing: English clubs would be readmitted to Europe in 1990/91. Hooliganism was still a problem, but after the Hillsborough disaster and Taylor Report, all-seater stadiums came into force.

With more family sections and kids and women going to games, the whole atmosphere changed. The Premier League would start in 1992, ushering an era of multimillion-pound transfer fees and salaries. More foreign players came to the UK, with only a handful playing in England before the World Cup.

The 1990 World Cup was also the most heavily promoted tournament ever at the time. As well as the Panini World Cup sticker collection, a famous collection called *World Cup 90* came out. It was a huge binder with 24 parts, each containing previews, World Cup history and team pages with action stickers for all 24 teams. I still have my completed binder somewhere. I used to get *Shoot!* and *Match* magazines and still have some copies from 1990. The post-tournament *World Soccer* review was a must, as it is after every World Cup and Euros.

A video collection was also released called *The World Cup Story*. It featured VHS tapes on England, Scotland, Brazil, Argentina, West Germany, Italy, the Netherlands, Spain, USSR, Uruguay and the contenders. I still have the Scotland VHS, which was presented by Andy Gray with commentary by Jock Brown. It showed every goal by Scotland in the World Cup finals from 1954 to 1986. It also featured interviews with Denis Law, David Hay, Alan Rough, Graeme Souness, Alex Ferguson and Andy Roxburgh. It previewed the tournament and discussed the squad that may go to Italy. In the closing credits Denis Law said, ' Costa Rica, we'll beat them!' Little did we know.

The 2-1 victory over Sweden put Scotland in a great position. They knew that a draw and a point against Brazil would take them into the second round for the first time at a World Cup. The South Americans had beaten Costa Rica 1-0 in their second game and with victory over Sweden they had already qualified for the knockout rounds with four points. Would they change their team and rest players to face Scotland? How motivated would they be? For Roxburgh and Craig Brown the Brazil game would give them a huge dilemma. I think both were instinctively cautious and defensive, so the temptation to pack the team with defenders and play for a draw was obvious. However, without a goal threat of their own, it seemed impossible for Scotland to keep a clean sheet against Brazil.

The Sweden game was very emotional and draining, and with only four days before the Brazil match, Roxburgh would have to make changes. He also had to consider making changes to the system. They had played most of their pre-World Cup friendlies in a 3-5-2 formation. Would it be against Brazil where they played with three centre-backs?

There was a lot of talk in the British media and press about the continental sweeper system. Mark Wright had performed admirably as England gained a valuable point in a 0-0 draw with the Netherlands, on the same night that Scotland beat Sweden. Bobby Robson had learned from a 3-1 defeat to the Dutch at Euro 88, where Marco van Basten scored a hat-trick. With Terry Butcher, Des Walker and Wright, Van Basten and Ruud Gullit were nullified. The game also saw the emergence of Paul Gascoigne, who was outstanding. Italia 90 was truly the start of Gazzamania.

18

So Near Yet So Far

20 June 1990 – Scotland v Brazil

THE LEGEND of Brazil goes back to Pelé and 1958, when the 17-year-old dazzled the world as the *Seleção* won the World Cup for the first time, in Sweden. They retained the trophy four years later in Chile, then their third World Cup win in 1970 was their greatest. To this day they are regarded as the best Brazil team of all time and to many people as the greatest team ever to win the World Cup. They finished fourth in 1974 and third in 1978, the latter controversially as there was talk of a fix with Argentina thrashing Peru and their Buenos Aires-born goalkeeper 6-0 to deny Brazil a place in the final against the Netherlands on goal difference.

I think the 1982 group was their best since 1970. They played brilliant attacking football but lost 3-2 to Italy in an epic quarter-final. Despite that defeat, Telê Santana's team were hailed by many as the best team never to win the World Cup. In 1986 they returned to Mexico, scene of their most recent triumph; Santana was back as coach but the team was ageing and lacked the flair of Spain 1982. They opted for a more European-style sweeper system and were unlucky to go out in the quarter-final to European champions France on penalties, after another epic game, having only conceded one goal in five games. In 1990 they were among the favourites to win the trophy, but the Brazilian press were very critical, despite the fact that coach Sebastião Lazaroni had recently led Brazil to the 1989 Copa América, their first triumph since 1949.

There were some famous names in their squad for the 1990 finals: Cláudio Taffarel would go on to be arguably Brazil's greatest ever goalkeeper and at the time of writing was a goalkeeping coach at Liverpool; defensive midfielder Dunga would captain Brazil to victory at the 1994 World Cup in the USA; Romário would only start one game in Italy; Bebeto played just seven minutes as a substitute in the whole tournament. They relied on Napoli striker Careca who had just won the 1989/90 Serie A title alongside Diego Maradona. The team lacked width and, apart from Müller too, it was hard to see where the goals would come from.

Brazil breezed through qualification, easily getting the better of Chile and Venezuela. Chile goalkeeper Roberto Rojas was banned for life (later lifted in 2001) after he had left the pitch on a stretcher during the qualification game in Rio. It was later discovered that he had not been hit by a firework but that he had cut himself with a razor blade hidden in his glove.

Chile refused to complete the game and FIFA awarded Brazil a 2-0 victory. Chile were also banned from the 1994 World Cup.

Brazil embarked on a series of glamour friendlies in the build-up to Italy, with some notable successes. They beat the hosts 1-0 in Bologna in October 1989, then in December they beat European champions the Netherlands 1-0 in

Rotterdam. In March 1990 they were beaten 1-0 by England at Wembley, to a Gary Lineker goal, although the game is largely remembered for Stuart Pearce blocking the ball on the line with his hand, but the referee not awarding the penalty.

Lazaroni favoured a sweeper system and the 1990 team was noted for its physical strength but a lack of creativity. They were certainly missing flair compared to Brazil teams of the past, but the coach believed the European style could win the World Cup in Europe. He felt that their traditional skill would be exposed by other European sides. He seemed to be a cautious coach and, looking back, it is hard to understand why he did not play Romário or Bebeto more, especially when that strike force would lead Brazil to glory four years later.

For their final decisive group game, Scotland moved from their base in Rapello near Genoa to St Vincent near Turin, where they would face Brazil. St Vincent, in the Aosta Valley, was about 2,000ft above sea level and much cooler than the humid climes of Rapello. The Stadio Delle Alpi, newly built for the World Cup, would host the game: with a capacity of 68,000, it was the home of Juventus and Torino, although it was soulless, exposed to the elements with poor views and unpopular with fans. It would eventually be demolished in 2009 and replaced by the 41,000-capacity Juventus Stadium.

On 20 June 1990 it had been raining all day as the players got to the Stadio Delle Alpi before the 9pm local time kick-off. Stuart McCall recalled to the BBC in 2022, 'I remember arriving at the stadium and both buses arrived together. The Brazilians were being mobbed by all these dancing beauties and we had the Tartan Army offering us swigs of lager.'

Brazil had been impressive in their 1-0 victory over Costa Rica on 16 June. They attacked from the start and were desperately unlucky, hitting the woodwork several times. Some brilliant saves by Gabelo Conejo meant that only a deflected goal by Müller from a throw-in separated the sides.

On ITV before the match, a nervous Andy Roxburgh said, 'This for us of course is a vitally important game, we could break a barrier here. Very few people give us a chance of being in the finals, and then once we got here, few people gave us a chance of being in with a chance. But we've got that, we've got that opportunity. And therefore we go into the match on a high and we'll do our utmost to try and make sure that we get into the next phase.'

Huge screens were erected in the city so that Scottish fans without tickets could see the game. Roxburgh was grateful for all the support, 'We anticipate that about 10,000 of the crowd will be our own, but you know 10,000 Scotsman can sound like 50,000. So it will be a bit of a competition off the park as well as on it.'

Roxburgh was expecting a different style of match than against Sweden, 'Somehow, I don't think it will be as frantic and that is simply because the Brazilians won't want to play that kind of game. They'll want to keep possession and build the thing carefully and play it at their own tempo. And it will be up to us to try and dictate the pace as best we possibly can.'

On the chance to make history by leading Scotland to the second round for the first time, he said, 'You can look at anything in terms of pressure, but you can also look at it in a positive way, it's a positive challenge.'

When the teams were announced, Roxburgh had sprung a surprise. He had opted for a 3-5-2 formation, but for the first time since he'd been in charge, he chose captain Roy Aitken to be the third central defender. Aitken had played most of his career at centre-back for Celtic but since he returned to the Scotland team in 1985, he had been used as a defensive midfielder. Given that Roxburgh had used 3-5-2 in several of the pre-tournament friendlies, it was strange that he had never selected Aitken in that position in any of those matches. Craig Levein, so impressive against Sweden, was injured and Stewart McKimmie returned to the side. Gordon Durie and Robert Fleck dropped out and Ally McCoist started for the first time at the World Cup.

McCoist was delighted, as he told talkSPORT in 2022, 'Now you may think I would say this anyway, but I think Andy picked the wrong team against Costa Rica. It is as simple as that. If he had played me alongside Mo, it might have been different. I honestly do. It might have made all the difference at the start of the campaign. That first game was vital. It could have put us on the right road. Put in this way, was I more likely to score against Brazil than I was against Costa Rica or even Sweden? I don't think so.'

He recalled the game, 'I didn't think Brazil were at their best but, on the other hand, I can't recollect an international I have played in where we've had so little possession. What did surprise me was that although they were brilliant technically, there was a lack of urgency about the way they played. I don't know. They just looked easy on the ball but without any real bite. And let's not forget they could defend and they were tough.'

As I prepared to watch live on ITV, I couldn't say I was confident, but I felt that we could get a draw. The team showed that they were capable of a solid defensive performance in the 1-0 friendly win over Argentina in

March. However, there had been major problems in defence in qualifying and in the run-up to the World Cup. The three goals lost to Yugoslavia, three in France and the one at home to Norway were all avoidable. Scotland had also conceded three to Egypt in May as well as the crazy Gary Gillespie own goal at home to Poland. They could not even keep a clean sheet in Malta, though they did scrape a 2-1 win a few weeks before the World Cup.

Given that in most of the friendlies the 3-5-2 formation was not successful, I was a bit shocked that Roxburgh chose to face Brazil with that setup. Also Roy Aitken was not known for his pace and had never played as a sweeper under Roxburgh before. I did take some comfort from the fact that Brazil had already won the group and would clearly make changes. I did not think they would be as motivated as if the game was one they had to win to make the knockout stages. It was clearly not the greatest Brazilian team either, and having watched them beat Sweden and Costa Rica by one goal each, they did not seem very prolific. I took heart that they did not possess a team with the superstars of the past. No Sócrates, Zico, Éder, who I had watched destroy us in 1982 as a kid growing up in Glasgow.

With the huge downpour, I thought the wet conditions would suit Scotland more. In all the World Cups and Euros I'd seen from 1982 to 2024, I had often felt that we would find it difficult to score goals, especially at the European Championships of 1992, 1996, 2020 and 2024. I never had any worries in 1982, when we scored eight goals in three games. In 1986 we were in a very tough group and the problems up front were there for all to see. We only scored one goal in three games, and that was by Gordon Strachan, a midfielder. Despite having some very good strikers on paper, like Charlie Nicholas, Frank McAvennie, Graeme Sharp, Paul Sturrock and Steve Archibald, we rarely looked like finding the back of the net. At the 1998 World Cup, despite Kevin Gallacher hitting six in qualifying, goals were again hard to come by – only two in three games, which makes it even harder to understand why Craig Brown did not select Ally McCoist in his squad. He later apologised to Ally and told him he had made a mistake.

In 1990, with McCoist and Mo Johnston, I always felt confident that we could score. For me, between 1988 and 1990 Johnston was one of the top strikers in Europe. He had also come off the back of an excellent season at Rangers, winning the 1989/90 Scottish league championship. Very impressive when you consider all the pressure and spotlight he was under as the first Catholic to sign at Ibrox. Ally was a great foil for Mo, which made it even more surprising that Roxburgh did not start him until the last and hardest group game, against Brazil.

In midfield, Paul McStay had always seemed to frustrate me. I saw his performances for Celtic week in and week out on TV. There was no doubt that he was a class player, he had skill and vision and the ability to run a game and score goals, but apart from his early years when he broke into the team as an 18-year-old in 1983, he seemed to shrink when he pulled on a Scotland shirt.

He was anonymous against Uruguay in the 1986 World Cup, although there were some notable performances, such as when he was excellent in the 2-0 win over Belgium in 1987 and outstanding in the 2-0 victory against France in 1989. I always felt, given his ability, that he should have scored more goals for his country. Maybe, at Italia 90 he could finally show what he could do on the world stage.

In defence, I always felt that Richard Gough was a world-class player. It surprised me that from 1983 to 1990 he was mostly used at right-back. In my opinion, his best position was at centre-back, as shown by his outstanding partnership with Terry Butcher at Rangers.

Alex McLeish was always rock solid, and although I'd always rated Willie Miller, at 35, even if he had been fit, I doubt that Roxburgh would have selected him in his 1990 squad. Maurice Malpas was always sound and reliable, but I felt it was a big blow that Steve Nicol had to pull out injured just before the World Cup. He was so versatile and able to play in any position in defence and midfield.

One of the most interesting choices, I felt, was in goal. I always rated Jim Leighton, whose Scotland record was incredible: 45 clean sheets in 91 games. But by 1990 he was not at his best and lacking in confidence. To be dropped from the FA Cup Final just a few weeks before the World Cup would have been a devastating blow to him. I felt that Andy Goram should have got the nod in Italy. He had been very impressive in the build-up and for Hibs throughout the 1989/90 season. Andy Roxburgh was a loyal man and, looking back, I don't think there was any chance that he would have dropped Leighton. However, we saw in 1978 what happened when Ally MacLeod selected Don Masson and Bruce Rioch, both in bad club form, for the World Cup. Neither of them played for Scotland again after Argentina.

I was not one of the critics of Roy Aitken, with many in the press calling for him to be dropped. For me, he was an inspirational figure. I also rated Jim Bett highly. I think he should have started in the 1986 World Cup, but despite his Aberdeen manager Alex Ferguson being in charge, he did not play at all. On paper, Scotland's 1990 squad lacked the big names and world-class players from the past – no Danny McGrain, Graeme Souness or Kenny Dalglish – but they were close-knit and the harmony between the players made them a tight unit.

Maurice Malpas explained to the BBC Sport website in 2020, 'I think we had a side that could have gone further in competition. We were pretty much the same squad game by game and I think compared to my previous finals in Mexico, we were a group of journeymen international players. I don't mean that in a bad way. It's just that we didn't have a world-class star like Kenny Dalglish or Graeme Souness this time. We did have excellent players but nobody was Billy big time, it was a combined effort.

'We got on well together and that wasn't an accident. We were tight-knit and all the better because of that. When Roxy took over Scotland, he made the point of splitting up the cliques. No longer were there Anglos, west coast and east coast. With our group from the east often the biggest in terms of numbers. Everyone mixed more in Italy and that was the real achievement for the management team at the time. Looking back, it was a wonderful experience to play at that level for your country.'

The injured Craig Levein recalled to *The Scotsman* in 2020, 'We went into the Brazil game with confidence because of the way we performed and the fact we beat Sweden. There were key moments in the Brazil game and had they gone our way, we could have won that. If we got through, it would have been an amazing situation. We were genuinely very close to doing it.'

Maurice Malpas told the *Courier Evening Telegraph* in 2020, 'The thing that stands out for me was that it was a really tight game and I guess that is a compliment to

Scotland. We had thought beforehand that we could get something from it and that confidence stayed with us for almost the whole match.'

Scotland lined up as follows:

Leighton

McPherson–Aitken (c)–McLeish

McKimmie–McCall–McStay–MacLeod (Gillespie 39)–Malpas

McCoist (Fleck 77)–Johnston

Brazil kicked off in a rain-soaked Turin, with Brian Moore and Billy McNeill commentating for ITV. The opening stages were bogged down in midfield. The Austrian referee Helmut Kohl booked Mo Johnston and Murdo MacLeod early on, for me quite harshly. He was constantly blowing for fouls even with minimal contact, so there was no early flow to the game. Jorginho looked a threat overlapping on the right, and the first clear chance came after ten minutes, but Branco's free kick from 25 yards was driven wide.

Aitken looked comfortable and his run from the back earned a free kick on the halfway line, but Brazil almost took the lead when Jorginho crossed from the right and McKimmie headed behind for a corner. Leighton flicked it away and after 15 minutes there was no score. It was vital that McStay and McCall kept the ball in midfield, to keep the pressure off the Scotland defence. Brazil opened them up a few minutes later, however. Dunga fired a great crossfield ball with the outside of his foot and Alemão's cross was scrambled behind. McCoist and Johnston looked isolated up front; Scotland's first foray into the Brazil area led to nothing as Johnston's cross aimed for McCoist was headed clear. Roxburgh ideally wanted McKimmie and Malpas to give the Scots width, but they rarely got forward and just stayed in position, so that without the ball Scotland were effectively in a 5-3-2 setup. Alemão had a free kick on the edge of the Scotland area, but drove the ball straight at the wall. From the corner, Leighton punched clear and it came to nothing.

On 26 minutes Branco blasted a free kick off the side of Murdo MacLeod's head. He was knocked out and dazed and confused. The Brazilians were playing within themselves with a slow build-up to their attacks. They did look like they could step up a gear if they needed to. Romário did not look fit after returning from a broken leg in March. He had netted an incredible 51 goals in 52 games for his Dutch club PSV and had also scored seven goals as Brazil had finished as runners-up at the 1988 Seoul Olympics. Alemão fired well wide as Scotland grew more and more into the game, then Dunga drove a free kick wide and the Scots defended well from a series of corners.

On 39 minutes MacLeod went off. Gary McAllister had been warming up but Roxburgh threw on Gary Gillespie, who replaced Aitken as sweeper with the Newcastle man moving back into midfield. Gillespie had a chance to put in a sound defensive display after his own goal in the warm-up game at home to Poland. The Scots were staying compact and in their shape with Stewart McKimmie having a superb game, excellent on the ball and strong in the tackle.

Malpas also looked solid and McCall and McStay looked composed on the ball. At half-time Scotland had held firm and it was 0-0; Roxburgh's men were just 45 minutes away from the knockout stages for the first time in their history.

Scotland kicked off the second half and although I don't think they would not consciously play for a draw, the longer the game went on the more they were likely to sit back and defend. A promising lay-off by McCoist set up McStay on the edge of the box, but Brazil scrambled the ball clear. Leighton then saved Romário's header from a corner at the other end. The movement by Brazil in the final third always looked threatening, but Scotland kept their shape well. They needed to keep more possession to take the sting out of the game, however.

Almost on the hour, Romário was played through on the edge of the box, but Leighton made a superb save diving at his feet. After a fine passing move McCall fed McCoist running through the Brazil defence, but his touch was heavy and the ball was cleared. On 65 minutes Torino striker Müller replaced Romário as Scotland began to retreat deeper and deeper and constantly played the ball back to Leighton. With 20 minutes left Careca fired over from the edge of the area with Brazil seeming content not to throw many men forward and lacking a bit of urgency. Scotland needed McStay and Aitken to keep hold of the ball to relieve the pressure. So far, McLeish, Gillespie and McPherson had coped admirably against the Brazilian forwards. Watching at home on the TV was very nerve-wracking and the longer the game went on the more I started to believe we could get a 0-0 draw. But, as ever with Scotland, you always felt that you were a moment away from disaster too.

McStay fired a free kick from the left and the Scots forced a corner, but it came to nothing. A set piece looked like their best bet for a goal. Brazil threatened soon after on the left, but Leighton's handling was secure from a deep cross. Scotland then almost took the lead as McCall's corner was met by Aitken, but his powerful header was cleared off the line by Branco. With just 15 minutes left, Scotland began to sense that they could hold on for a priceless point. On 77 minutes Robert Fleck replaced a tired-looking Ally McCoist, then on 81 minutes McStay gave the ball away. Alemão shot from the edge of the box, Leighton could only parry it, as Gillespie and Careca scrambled for the rebound, and Müller followed up to score from a tight angle. Alex McLeish was slow to react and just stood and watched. I think Leighton should have held the shot or parried it wide of the goal instead of into the central danger area.

That old familiar sinking feeling came over me once again. It was cruel on Scotland but as ever they needed one more goal in their final World Cup game to qualify for the second round. They could not find one in 1982 in a 2-2 draw with the Soviet Union and in 1986 in a 0-0 draw with Uruguay. So what chance could they find a late goal in 1990?

Leighton fumbled the ball soon afterwards but it was scrambled clear; once again the decision of Roxburgh not to choose the in-form Andy Goram looked like a big mistake. His loyalty to Leighton had backfired. Buoyed by their goal, Brazil pressed forward and McPherson had to head the ball behind under pressure at the back post. Brazil now had the bit between their teeth and had clearly stepped up a gear. From a Scotland corner Brazil broke and Leighton did well to save Alemão's powerful drive.

In the 91st minute McKimmie pumped a high ball into the box. McCall headed it down, Fleck miskicked and it fell to Mo Johnston inside the six-yard box. He met it firmly and the ball was arrowing into the top corner but somehow Taffarel flung himself to tip the shot over. It was an unbelievable save; for me, the save of the tournament so far. Johnston collapsed on the ground with his head in his hands. Scotland had literally been a fingertip away from making history. The final whistle blew a few seconds later to give Brazil a 1-0 victory.

I shed a tear after I realised we were out. There was a very slim chance Scotland could make it through if a series of results went their way but they didn't. Uruguay beat South Korea in injury time and the Netherlands and Republic of Ireland played out a 1-1 draw, knowing that the point would take them both through. Even if results had gone their way, with Austria also on two points, the drawing of lots would have been required. Scotland would probably have lost that as well.

In his 2000 autobiography *In The Firing Line*, Jim Leighton said, 'We were on level terms with only eight minutes to go when a shot from Alemão bounced in front of me and came off the ground quickly. It hit me and broke away to create a scramble. I thought one of our defenders might have managed to come to the rescue, but it was not to be. Müller profited from the situation to score the only goal of the game. I was blamed for the loss of that goal and offer no excuses. It was a goalkeeping error that had opened the door to Brazil, and it took me a long time to get over it. I stayed on the pitch after the final whistle. The thought in my mind was that it would be my last appearance in the World Cup finals.

'As well as dwelling on my error, I wanted to look around me and remember what playing at that level had been like. The Brazilian goalkeeper Cláudio Taffarel came all the way from the other end to console me. He spoke very little English and I had no Portuguese, but we understood each other. Only another goalkeeper knows how lonely you can feel in such circumstances, and I much appreciated his gesture. I'd made one mistake in three games. But it was one too many.'

Mo Johnston told the BBC post~-match, 'Very disappointed. That's a few chances I've had in the World Cup. I scored the penalty kick [the winner against Sweden in the previous match]. The goalkeeper made honestly an unbelievable save from me in the last minute. And I just feel sorry for the fans. There's 10,000 out there and obviously they'll go home very, very disappointed, because, let's face it, we gave so much tonight and got so little.'

In the 1994 STV documentary *Faith, Hope and Calamity*, Johnston explained, 'When you hit the target, that's all you can ask for from a striker. For me it was hitting the top corner, it's hit the top of his shoulder. Nine times out of ten they go in, but that's the way things go. In the past they've went in, this time they never.'

In 2018 he said in *Adventures in the Golden Age*, 'Dying seconds and I miss a sitter. I smashed it and what do you know, it touches the top of Taffarel's shoulder, rises up and goes over. Yes it was his shoulder but it must go down as a great save. I just lay there thinking our World Cup is over. That's the one I always think about, it never goes away.'

Paul McStay told the BBC post-match, 'It's very disappointing, especially after the first game, a game we had all the ball, created all the chances and just couldn't win it. Then the Sweden game the lads went down, put in a great performance, got two thoroughly deserved points. And then tonight a wee bit unfortunate. Overall, I think the first game messed it up a wee bit for us.'

Twenty-four hours after the defeat, Andy Roxburgh reflected to BBC Scotland, 'Well, no one said life was fair and sometimes you have to take the blows. And, let's be honest, we lost to a better side, the Brazilians have a bit of magic about them. But we worked diligently throughout the game. We had to play in a very practical way, face up to reality. And it really was a cruel blow to lose out just at the death as we did. Particularly to such a soft goal. I felt last night we had to get the point to qualify. We didn't get the point. Everything is in other people's hands now. We will just watch the events unfold. I don't think the odds are very good.'

For Tartan Army regulars Alex and Stuart McLean, it had been a sad end to a memorable day.

Alex said, 'The weather was awful all day in Turin. We got on well with the Brazil fans but I did not like the stadium. It was miles out of town. I knew we couldn't beat Brazil but I thought we could nick a draw. We were surprised Roxburgh went 3-5-2 with big Roy as sweeper but he did well. The longer the game went on, the more stressed I got. We almost made it but Brazil were the better side. In the last second when the ball fell to wee Mo, we jumped up and screamed, "Goal!" but I still don't know how Taffarel kept it out. It was another hard-luck story, but Scotland did us proud against Sweden and Brazil.

'We flew home the next day as we knew the other results would not go for us. I enjoyed the trip and, looking back 35 years later, it was amazing to see us mix with the likes of Brazil. We expected to qualify for the World Cup back then. I saw us play Brazil at the opening game of the 1998 World Cup too. It was a great occasion. I didn't dream that would be the last World Cup Scotland went to.'

Stuart added, 'We saw all three games. The Sweden game still gives me goosebumps. Overall, I think we played as well as we could, but nerves in the first game against

Costa Rica affected us. I think we would have won if Roxburgh started McCoist and Johnston together, but their keeper was unbeatable that day. I felt sorry for Jim Leighton, but he should have held that shot against Brazil.

'Although people said it was one of the worst squads we ever sent to the World Cup, we had some top-class players. To this day I've not seen a better pair of strikers than Mo Johnston and Ally McCoist. Kenny Dalglish was a wee bit before my time. It was a great summer and still my favourite World Cup, although I'll admit I really thought England could win it!'

* * *

How would 1990 rate among Scotland's World Cups in a row? For me, the 1974 squad was the best we ever took to a World Cup. It was the most balanced and as a result proved the most successful, in that they were unbeaten in all three games, with a notable 0-0 draw with world champions Brazil. The team only conceded one goal in three games. However, only scoring twice against Zaire when the Yugoslavs hit nine and Brazil three ultimately proved decisive. Scotland became the first team in World Cup history to be eliminated undefeated.

In 1978 Scotland sent a side packed with some top players to Argentina, but mistakes on and off the park contributed to a disaster. The accommodation was terrible, and I think Ally MacLeod picked the wrong squad. Gordon McQueen was selected even though he was not fit enough to play in any of the three games. For me, leaving Andy Gray at home was a huge mistake. MacLeod never watched Peru play, and despite detailed reports by Andy Roxburgh, the team were not prepared to face the Copa América holders.

I think he consistently chose the wrong starting 11. For me, Graeme Souness should have started all three games.

After his awful mistake against Iran, when he was beaten at his near post, I think Alan Rough should have been dropped. Willie Johnston taking a banned hay fever medication could not have been predicted even in MacLeod's worst nightmare. With the Scottish league's top scorer Derek Johnstone on the bench, and a winner required against Iran, MacLeod sent on Joe Harper instead. For me, it made no sense. The Rangers striker was the man in form. He had scored against Northern Ireland and a brilliant header against Wales in the build-up to the World Cup. Scotland were then unfortunate to lose to England at Hampden. After an excellent performance they could find no way past a stubborn defence and, a few minutes from the end, Rough dropped the ball to Steve Coppell who scored the only goal.

Looking back, I believe the decision by the SFA secretary Ernie Walker to hold a send-off at Hampden before the players departed for Argentina was also a bad idea. MacLeod claimed later that he did not want to attend a victory parade before the team left for the World Cup, but Walker insisted. The money raised went to the redevelopment of Hampden Park and the 30,000 fans got the chance to wave the players off before they flew to South America.

Controversy still rages to this day whether Ally MacLeod announced that Scotland would win the 1978 World Cup. He did say that if they played to form and had some luck, they could come back home with a medal. That meant as a finalist or the third-placed team. I think, when MacLeod did pick the right team in that last game, they showed what they could do. Outplaying finalists, the Netherlands, the 3-2 victory did not do the Scots justice: they had a good goal wrongly disallowed and hit the woodwork. Archie Gemmill scored the most famous goal in Scotland history; his brilliant mazy run showed the world what the team could do, but sadly it was too little too late. Had Jock Stein been in charge in 1978, everything could have been so different. I think he was too experienced to make the same mistakes MacLeod did.

However, it is worth pointing out how successful MacLeod was in his first year in charge. A 2-1 win at Wembley retained the British Home Championship, the Scots' first win at Wembley since 1967. The Tartan Army celebrated by invading the pitch, tearing down the crossbar and digging up the turf. Scotland then had a successful South American tour, beating Chile 4-2, earning a 1-1 draw in Argentina and losing 2-0 to Brazil in Rio. A 3-1 victory over European champions Czechoslovakia at Hampden helped seal a place at the 1978 World Cup. So it could be argued that Scotland peaked a year too soon, and had the tournament taken place in 1977, they would have done far better. Despite his flaws, I think MacLeod was a good man, honest if naive, and those 18 months were some of the most exciting times the Tartan Army ever had.

In 1982 Jock Stein seemed like the right man at the right time. Scotland had qualified impressively, topping their group ahead of Northern Ireland, who made it to the second group stage. The preparations were thorough, the accommodation far better and Stein had watched each opponent and thoroughly prepared the team to face them. The 1982 squad had world-class players, many with European medals. George Burley, John Wark and Alan

Brazil were UEFA Cup winners with Ipswich. Allan Evans was a European Cup winner with Aston Villa, while Frank Gray and John Robertson had won it with Nottingham Forest, as had Alan Hansen, Graeme Souness and Kenny Dalglish at Liverpool.

However, I think Jock Stein picked the wrong team in all three matches. He didn't pick Aberdeen duo Willie Miller and Alex McLeish together. Hansen and Evans were poor in the 5-2 win over New Zealand where those two bad goals conceded would cost Scotland a place in the next round. Stein stuck with Hansen in the next two games, but he could not play effectively with Miller. After being thrashed 4-1 by Brazil, Scotland faced the Soviet Union in their final group game. There was a rerun of the full match in 2020 on BBC Scotland. An excellent performance was ruined by a comical error in the last few minutes. Hansen ran into Miller and striker Ramaz Shengelia raced through to score the decisive goal. Despite a late equaliser by captain Graeme Souness, the 2-2 draw was not enough and, for the third World Cup in a row, Scotland were eliminated on goal difference.

Stein's decisions seemed to make little sense. The night before the USSR game he asked his coaches to write down what team they would select. Assistant Jim McClean and Andy Roxburgh spent hours selecting their starting 11, before presenting their team sheet to Stein. Without looking, he ripped up the piece of paper and said, 'Och, I'll just pick the team myself.' After telling his staff he would drop Alan Rough after his performance against Brazil, he selected him to face the Soviets. Having dropped Kenny Dalglish from the starting line-up against Brazil, Stein did not even select the Liverpool man on the bench against the USSR.

For me that was a terrible mistake. Dalglish was feared by his opponents and his skill and experience at turning tight European defences could have made all the difference. To this day it is hard to understand why Stein dropped him.

For once, Scotland hadn't had any problem scoring goals: they hit eight in three games. However, they conceded eight too. Only El Salvador, who lost 10-1 to Hungary, conceded more in the first phase.

By 1986 Stein had tragically died and his assistant and Aberdeen manager Alex Ferguson was at the helm. Again I think he selected the wrong squad. I was not surprised that Alan Hansen missed out, as he had not started any of the qualifiers, and it seemed as though Ferguson decided to punish him for pulling out of the squad to face England at Wembley in April. His contempt for the Liverpool defender was clear in his 2000 autobiography *Managing My Life*, admitting that he 'simply felt that he [Hansen] did not deserve to go to Mexico'.

Ferguson wrote, 'Nobody with any sense could ever doubt Alan Hansen's quality as a central defender, but his tendency to pull out of Scotland matches had raised a question in my mind about his reliability and perhaps his attitude. His deserved reputation as a marvellous player was based on his achievements with Liverpool. I have to say that, to me, he was never as remarkable with Scotland.

'We were training at Luton's ground in April 1986 before the England game at Wembley. However, Alan walked up to my assistant Walter Smith and said, "I can feel my knee, I'll need to go back." Then without any real discussion he left for Liverpool. I felt instantly that it was all too much of a re-run of the episode in Cardiff, when his late withdrawal so annoyed Jock Stein.'

Scotland were once again drawn in a very tough group – with 1982 World Cup finalists West Germany, Copa América holders Uruguay, and the in-form Europeans Denmark appearing at their first World Cup finals.

Goals would be at a premium but Ferguson did not select his best striker and the top scorer in UEFA qualifying, Mo Johnston. His two goals had seen off Euro 84 finalists Spain 3-1 at Hampden, on a memorable night when Kenny Dalglish's brilliant goal equalled Denis Law's Scotland record of 30. Ferguson explained in his autobiography that Johnston was left out for his off-field exploits. In Australia for the World Cup play-off, he had a woman in his room. Mo was a single man, but it was unprofessional the night before a game. Johnston apologised and a line should have been drawn. But, once again, I think it seemed Ferguson decided to punish the Celtic striker. Ally McCoist had hit 28 goals and was the SPL's top scorer. He made an impressive debut in a 0-0 draw in the Netherlands but was not selected. Ferguson picked Paul Sturrock, who had not played in any of the qualifiers and had not scored for Scotland since 1982. When Dalglish pulled out injured a few days after the 1986 FA Cup Final victory, which gave Liverpool the league and cup double, Ferguson had a big problem. He replaced him with the half-fit Barcelona striker Steve Archibald, who had not scored for Scotland since a header in the win over New Zealand at the 1982 World Cup.

For the decisive game against Uruguay, Ferguson dropped captain Graeme Souness, against the advice of his assistant Walter Smith. He later admitted it was a bad mistake, as, without his powerful presence, the Scots were intimidated and kicked out of the World Cup by their violent opponents. He did not pick Jim Bett in any of the games;

he said later that he did not want to be accused of favouring Aberdeen players. I think Ferguson was too inexperienced and it showed. He resigned within an hour of the 0-0 draw with Uruguay. We should have known it was Friday the 13th! With only three victories in ten games, Ferguson had one of the worst win records of any Scotland boss.

In 1990 the preparation was faultless. Scotland had booked their accommodation early and the players enjoyed being based in Rapello. As befitted two teachers, Roxburgh and his assistant Craig Brown had done their homework. They organised a pre-tournament training camp in Genoa in February 1990. I think Roxburgh picked the right squad, but his loyalty to Jim Leighton proved very costly. It would have been a bold and brave decision to drop him and play Andy Goram, but I think that Goram would not have made the same error against Brazil.

I think there is no doubt Roxburgh picked the wrong line-up against Costa Rica. If he had selected Mo Johnston and Ally McCoist from the start, and the team played their normal game, I am convinced that they would have secured at least a draw with the Central Americans. That would have been enough to see Scotland through to the knockout stages.

I think he left it too late to bring McCoist on, waiting until the 73rd minute. The perceived weakness of Costa Rica in the air was evident when they were thrashed 4-1 by Czechoslovakia in the last 16: Tomáš Skuhravý scored a hat-trick of headers. Scotland were very unlucky and Costa Rica scored from their only shot on target in the whole match. However, Roxburgh knew how vital the opening game was and how motivated Costa Rica would be to put in a performance. After an hour, I think he should have changed tactics from knocking long balls up to McInally and mixed it up. Playing with more width and getting crosses into the box might have made all the difference. It followed on from Scotland's history of falling down against so-called weaker nations. Was it a mentality issue? I think they never seemed to enjoy going into games as favourites.

Against Sweden, I think Roxburgh got everything right. For me, his team selection and tactics were spot on. The fact that it was a do-or-die clash helped focus the players' minds. Scotland went in as underdogs against the fancied Swedes. Roxburgh predicted that it would be like a British cup tie and packed his midfield accordingly. Craig Levein was superb and the strength and tackling of Murdo MacLeod and Stuart McCall was vital. Gordon Durie and Robert Fleck gave Scotland something different in attack, and that 2-1 win remains the Scots' last victory at a World Cup.

For the Brazil game, I think Scotland would always have gone in slightly overawed by their illustrious opponents. I think they would naturally have been looking for a draw, regardless of the results in their previous two matches. I felt Roxburgh and Brown were naturally cautious and defensive coaches, and they seemed to start every game with the intention of not losing and trying to win on the break, with the razor-sharp finishing of Mo Johnston or from set pieces. Scotland had been very impressive in winning four of their first five qualifiers but when the pressure was really on to get a point in Yugoslavia or in France, their defence collapsed.

It was hard to fault their performance against Brazil. Roy Aitken looked impressive as sweeper and Gary Gillespie slotted in well after MacLeod went off. In the final analysis, only a brilliant fingertip save by Taffarel from Mo Johnston prevented Scotland from making their own World Cup history. However, the Rangers striker was guilty of missing two clear-cut chances against Costa Rica. He was denied by Gabelo Conejo, whose performances would earn him a place in the World Cup squad of the tournament chosen by journalists. Had one of those efforts gone in, Scotland would have got at least a draw against Costa Rica. Roxburgh could not legislate for those misses and the clear header that Alan McInally put over in the same game. It was the Costa Rica match that proved decisive and it remains the most humiliating result in Scotland's history. The fact that they also beat Sweden 2-1 and only lost 1-0 to Brazil proved that they were a good team.

Costa Rica had a highly experienced manager in Bora Milutinović and the fact that they were unknown and appearing in their first World Cup proved a disadvantage for Scotland. I blame the awful white-and-yellow-striped away kit!

So, for me, 1990 was a near miss by Scotland rather than a glorious failure. It was arguably the weakest squad they had taken to a World Cup finals, but far stronger than the one Scotland sent to Euro 2024, their most recent tournament. In all positions, the 1990 team was stronger. Leighton and Goram were better goalkeepers than Angus Gunn, who was at fault in the opening 5-1 mauling by hosts Germany. McLeish, McPherson, Gough and Levein were all excellent defenders, far better than those available to Steve Clarke. In midfield, the 2024 side had the edge with the goal power of Scott McTominay and John McGinn and the skill and vision of Billy Gilmour. Roxburgh had Gary McAllister and John Collins and did not use either of them. I felt McAllister should have replaced Bett or McStay in the Costa Rica match.

Up front, Roxburgh had an embarrassment of riches compared to Clarke, whose options included Ché Adams and Lyndon Dykes. Both were good and honest players but hardly prolific. Yet Roxburgh did not choose what I felt was his best combination, of McCoist and Johnston, to start until the final game against Brazil, when he knew Scotland would have so little of the ball and chances would be few and far between. Roxburgh was right when he claimed that Scotland were unlucky at Italia 90, but the cold, hard truth was that they just weren't good enough. Good teams find a way to get results, even when they are not playing well. They also take their chances, which are at a premium at the highest level. Scotland were a good side but just not better than Brazil or Costa Rica on the day. They did their best and regained their pride with the win over Sweden. However, once again the latter stages were just beyond them.

19

Postscript

SCOTLAND AND Andy Roxburgh returned home to a muted reception. In August 1990 a special centenary match of the Scottish Football League took place at Hampden Park. A Scotland XI managed by Roxburgh took on a Scottish League XI managed by Jim McLean of Dundee United. Just 15,000 turned up to see the league win 1-0 with a penalty by Aberdeen striker Hans Gillhaus. Although it was just a friendly, it was an embarrassing defeat. The press were not impressed and Roxburgh was under pressure, but there was no time to dwell on that result as qualification for Euro 92 was about to start. At that time there were only eight teams in the finals: two groups of four with the top two in each group facing each other in the semi-finals, with the winners playing for the trophy.

Scotland had never qualified for the Euros and with a very tough group of Romania, Bulgaria, Switzerland and San Marino, the odds were against them making it to Sweden. Roxburgh had been in charge for four years and without an obvious replacement, he still had enough goodwill from the SFA to continue. However, he was expected to step down if Scotland failed to qualify for the finals.

The 1990 World Cup would see the swansong of several Scotland players as Roxburgh looked to rebuild for the Euro 92 qualifiers. Jim Leighton endured a torrid time after the World Cup, with loan spells at Arsenal where he didn't feature and even at Third Division Reading. Following an unhappy stint at Dundee, his career was revitalised when he signed for Hibs in 1993. He would win his first cap since Italia 90 in a 2-0 win in Malta in November 1993.

Andy Goram became the undisputed number one over the next four years, and the two friends would vie over the jersey until 1998. Goram was outstanding at Euro 92 and Euro 96, but Leighton was the first choice at France 1998 at the age of 39. He would retire later that year after appearing at three World Cups and travelling to four in total. His record of 91 caps leaves him second on the list of Scotland appearances, behind Kenny Dalglish, with 102 caps.

Bryan Gunn, despite his excellent form for Norwich, who would finish third in the 1992/93 Premier League, and famously beat Bayern Munich in the following season's UEFA Cup, never established himself in the team. He would win five more caps after the 1990 World Cup, with his final appearance in a 3-1 defeat in the Netherlands in 1994. He conceded ten goals in his six matches, keeping just one clean sheet.

Richard Gough would captain Scotland from 1990 to 1993 in his best position of centre-back. He was outstanding at Euro 92. After a 5-0 thrashing by Portugal in 1993, Gough announced his retirement. He had a difficult relationship with Andy Roxburgh and when Craig Brown replaced him at the end of 1993, Gough never played for Scotland again. Dave McPherson became the established partner for Gough and played at Euro 92, and he won his final cap in that 5-0 defeat in Portugal.

Maurice Malpas was a regular until the end of 1992, bowing out with 55 caps. Stewart McKimmie became a stalwart of the team for the next six years, with his final appearance against England at Euro 96. Craig Levein would play ten more times for his country, until 1994, earning a total of 16 caps. He had an ill-fated spell as Scotland manager from 2010 to 2012 as the national team failed to qualify for Euro 2012. He is best remembered for his infamous 4-6-0 formation in a 1-0 defeat in the Czech Republic. Gary Gillespie only played once more for his country before injuries and an unhappy spell at Celtic saw the end of his career. Captain Roy Aitken bowed out after Italia 90, telling Roxburgh that, at 32, he felt it was time to give younger players a chance. He earned one more cap, against Romania in October 1991, and would go on to be an assistant to Alex McLeish as Scotland boss in 2007.

Jim Bett never played for Scotland again; Stuart McCall, John Collins and Gary McAllister would become the mainstays of the midfield until 1999. McCall's last cap came just before the 1998 World Cup. He expected to go to the tournament but Craig Brown selected Paul Lambert instead. He had a fine career, earning 40 caps and playing in one World Cup and at Euro 92 and Euro 96. Collins was superb for Scotland, with his skill and vision a key feature, under Craig Brown especially. He was excellent at Euro 96 and will always be remembered for his equalising penalty against Brazil at the 1998 World Cup. His final game was a 1-0 win over England at Wembley in November 1999, in a Euro 2000 play-off second leg. He earned a total of 58 caps, scoring 12 goals. Gary McAllister would captain

Scotland with distinction from 1993 to 1997, retiring in 1999 after being booed by a section of supporters at Celtic Park, a minority never forgiving him for missing a penalty at Euro 96. I was there at Wembley on that sad afternoon. He earned 57 caps, scoring five goals. Paul McStay would play for Scotland until 1997; he was at his very best during the memorable Euro 92 campaign. He earned 76 caps, scoring nine goals. Murdo MacLeod earned his 20th and final cap in February 1991.

Up front, Robert Fleck did not win another cap after the 1990 World Cup and neither did Alan McInally. Mo Johnston retired after the World Cup but came back to play a few games at the end of 1991. After he left Rangers to join Everton in late 1991 he fell out of favour and was not part of the squad for Euro 92. Johnston's record of 14 goals in 38 games showed what a great finisher he was. Ally McCoist became the main striker after Italia 90, and would go on to score 19 goals in 61 games. Memorably, he scored Scotland's only goal at Euro 96. I was at Villa Park to see his brilliant strike beat Switzerland 1-0. Gordon Durie would go on to play until 1998: he would be the only player to appear at the 1990 World Cup, Euro 92, Euro 96 and the 1998 World Cup. Although he was a great team player and did a lot of hard running, he would only score seven goals in 43 games for Scotland.

What had Andy Roxburgh learned from the 1990 World Cup? The preparations were far better than in the past. The accommodation was excellent and the team were a strong collective unit, without the cliques of Anglos and homegrown players, Old Firm and the rest. That harmony was down to Roxburgh, Brown and their coaching staff. The tactical preparation was very high: Roxburgh always prepared his teams very well, with key information on their opponents.

However, looking back, I think he was too loyal to some players. For me, Jim Leighton should not have started all three games. I think Andy Goram was the better goalkeeper, confident and the man in form. I think Gary McAllister should have featured, especially against Costa Rica. While it is important to adapt when facing different opponents, Roxburgh completely altered Scotland's style of play when they faced Costa Rica. I don't think the team were used to pumping long, high balls into the box, and when it was clear that the strategy was not working, for me, Roxburgh should have brought on Ally McCoist after and hour, and swapped McAllister for Jim Bett. I think that would have made a big difference, but managers and coaches are defined by their team selections and I think Roxburgh picked the wrong team to face Costa Rica. I felt Mo Johnston and Ally McCoist should have started, and I think, had Scotland taken the lead, the whole outlook would have changed. Costa Rica would have had to come out and attack, and that could have suited Scotland. However, you can't legislate for missed chances and bad luck. Unfortunately for Scotland, Gabelo Conejo had the game of his life in the Costa Rica goal.

However, in the vital second match against Sweden, I think Roxburgh did a magnificent job of lifting the players and giving them the belief that they needed to beat the Scandinavians. He freshened up the team, and Levein, MacLeod, Durie and Fleck were excellent in the famous 2-1 victory. Come the Brazil game, Roxburgh knew that Scotland could not come out and attack. They did not have the players for that. I think his decision to play 3-5-2 with captain Roy Aitken as sweeper was inspired. When he moved Gary Gillespie to replace him, it again looked like a good decision. The Liverpool defender gave a calm and assured performance.

McStay gave the ball away but there seemed little danger when Alemão shot from the edge of the area. I think Leighton should have held the shot but he got to the rebound, as did Gillespie, but it was unfortunate that the ball spun away from both Scots and Careca to the unmarked Müller lurking at the far post. For me, Alex McLeish was too slow to react and he just stood and watched the Brazilian striker score. Roxburgh could do nothing about it but did try to get something from the game by sending on Fleck to replace the out-of-sorts McCoist. When the ball fell to Mo Johnston in injury time, he was the one man that you wanted, right in the middle of the six-yard box, with the goal at his mercy. He caught the ball well, hitting it hard towards the top corner. Taffarel instinctively threw himself and somehow tipped the shot over the bar. It was an unbelievable save, for me, the best of the tournament. I don't think there was anything more Mo Johnston could have done; it was agonising and it seemed desperately unlucky. However, it was Scotland's only shot on target in the game. Apart from a Roy Aitken header cleared off the line, they created nothing. Brazil always looked a threat and attacked throughout the 90 minutes.

One of the most disappointing things about Scotland at the 1990 World Cup was the performance of Paul McStay, who was poor against Costa Rica and anonymous against Brazil. Aitken had led the side well in all three games, but was not a creative player, or one who could score goals. Scotland lacked width and the full-backs Stewart McKimmie and Maurice Malpas rarely went forward.

Roxburgh seemed to favour solid, hard-working players like Murdo MacLeod and Stuart McCall, and although Gordon Durie had done quite well against Sweden, he was not a natural wide player.

Would Pat Nevin or Gordon Strachan have made a difference? I doubt that either of them would have started any game. Perhaps Davie Cooper could have unlocked tight defences, but Robert Fleck did well in attack in his place.

With little creativity from midfield, set pieces would be vital. Scotland had several free kicks on the edge of the area against Costa Rica, but failed to hit the target. McCall's goal against Sweden came from a well-worked and practiced corner routine. The victory against Sweden was all about pride, passion and battling qualities, against a team with many familiar players. Scotland were so motivated to put things right after the humiliation against Costa Rica that I think the players were always going to show a reaction. It was a glorious night and still the last time Scotland have won at a World Cup.

Overall, Scotland had decent spells in all three games, and watching back the full 90 against Costa Rica, they created several good chances. Nerves played a part; I think the players were cautious and keen not to give anything away. When they had chances to score, they found it difficult against a resolute defence. The Sweden victory was outstanding and great credit to Roxburgh and all the players. Against Brazil, I think a lack of belief, and maybe of confidence, was demonstrated by the players playing for a draw from the start of the second half. It was understandable that they didn't want to open up too much, as they feared the quality of the Brazilians, but sadly it was not to be in the end.

Andy Roxburgh would learn from Italia 90 and would take Scotland to Sweden in 1992, their first European Championship. There they would perform with great credit and enhance their reputation. Craig Brown would continue his good work in leading Scotland confidently to Euro 96 and the 1998 World Cup in France. The 1990s were truly a golden decade for the Scotland national team.

20

The 1990 World Cup
in Retrospect

FOR MANY people of a certain generation, Italia 90 remains the most memorable of all World Cups, with New Order's song 'World in Motion' and the BBC theme of Pavarotti's 'Nessun Dorma', which still evokes memories of that special summer. However, only 115 goals were scored in 52 games, an average of 2.21 per match, a record low that still stands. There were a then-record 16 red cards including two in the final. Italia 90 also held the record for the most penalty shoot-outs at a World Cup, four in the knockout stages including both semi-finals; that record wasn't beaten until 2022. Overly defensive tactics by many teams led to the introduction of the back-pass rule in 1992 and three points for a win in the 1994 finals.

Runners-up Argentina were prime examples of this trend of cautious defensive play, scoring only five goals in the entire tournament, a record low for a finalist. Argentina also became the first team to advance twice on penalty shoot-outs, the first team to fail to score in a final and the first to have a player sent off in a final.

Cameroon reached the quarter-finals, where they were narrowly defeated by England.

They opened the tournament with a shock victory over reigning champions Argentina, before topping the group ahead of of Romania, with Argentina in third place and Euro 1988 runners-up, the Soviet Union, bottom of the table. Their success was fired by the goals of Roger Milla, a 38-year-old striker who came out of international retirement to join the national squad at the last moment after a personal request from Cameroonian President Paul Biya. Milla's four goals and flamboyant celebrations made him one of the tournament's biggest stars. Most of Cameroon's squad was made up of players who played in France's Division 1, now called Ligue 1. In reaching this stage, they had gone further than any African nation had managed in a World Cup before; a feat not surpassed until Morocco reached the semi-final in 2022. Their success was African football's biggest yet on the world stage and FIFA subsequently decided to allocate the CAF qualifying zone an additional place for the next World Cup.

Hosts Italy won Group A with a 100 per cent record. They beat Austria 1-0 thanks to substitute Salvatore 'Totò' Schillaci, who had played only one international before but would become a star during the tournament. A second 1-0 victory followed against a USA side already thumped 5-1 by Czechoslovakia. The Czechs ended runners-up in the group, while the USA's first appearance in a World Cup since 1950 ended with three consecutive defeats.

In Group B Cameroon defeated world champions Argentina 1-0, despite ending the match with only nine men. There were contrasting fortunes for the Biyik brothers: François Omam-Biyik scoring the winning goal, shortly after seeing André Kana-Biyik sent off for a serious foul. In their second game the introduction of Milla was the catalyst for a 2-1 win over Romania, Milla scoring twice from the bench to become the World Cup's oldest goalscorer in a finals match.

Cameroon slumped to a 4-0 defeat in their final group game to the Soviet Union (in what would be their last World Cup). Argentina lost their veteran goalkeeper Nery Pumpido to a broken leg during their victory over the USSR: his replacement, Sergio Goycochea, proved to be one of the stars of their tournament. In the final match, a 1-1 draw between Romania and Argentina sent both through, equal on points and on goal difference but Romania having the advantage on goals scored: Romania were second and Argentina qualified as one of the best third-placed teams.

Group D featured the most goals of all the groups, primarily due to two large wins of West Germany and defensive inadequacies of a UAE team that lost 2-0 to Colombia, 5-1 to West Germany and 4-1 to Yugoslavia. The West Germans topped the group after a 4-1 opening victory over group runners-up Yugoslavia.

Spain topped Group E with Michel hitting a hat-trick as they beat South Korea 3-1 in an unbeaten group campaign. Belgium won their first two games, against South Korea and Uruguay, to ensure their progress; Uruguay's advance to the second round came with an injury-time winner against South Korea to edge them through as the weakest of the third-placed sides to remain in the tournament.

Group F featured the Netherlands, England, the Republic of Ireland and Egypt. No team managed to score more than once in any of the six matches. England beat Egypt 1-0, the only game with a decisive result, and that was enough to win the group. England took the lead with an early goal for Gary Lineker against Ireland, but Kevin Sheedy's late equaliser secured a draw. The Netherlands drew with Egypt: they had taken a 1-0 lead, but Egypt equalised with a penalty by Magdi Abdelghani. England then drew 0-0 with the Netherlands. Ireland could only manage a 0-0 draw against Egypt so, after the first four matches, all four teams had equal records with two draws, one goal for and one goal against. England's victory over Egypt, thanks to a 58th-minute header from Mark Wright, put them top of the group: in the other match, Ruud Gullit gave the the Netherlands the lead against Ireland, but Niall Quinn scored a second-half equaliser and the two teams finished in second and third, still with identical records. Both qualified but they had to draw lots to place the teams in second and third place.

* * *

In the last 16, Brazil v Argentina and Italy v Uruguay pitted former champions against each other, and West Germany met the Netherlands in a rematch of the 1974 World Cup Final. The all-South American game was won for Argentina by a goal from Claudio Caniggia with ten minutes remaining after a run through the Brazilian defence by Diego Maradona and a strong performance from their goalkeeper Sergio Goycochea. Italy beat Uruguay 2-0, thanks to goals from Schillaci and Aldo Serena.

The match between West Germany and the Netherlands was held in Milan, and both sides featured players from the two Milanese clubs: Germans Andy Brehme, Lothar Mattahus and Jürgen Klinsmann of Inter, and Dutchmen Marco van Basten, Ruud Gullit and Frank Rijkaard of AC Milan. After 22 minutes, Rudi Völler and Rijkaard were both sent off after a series of incidents between the two players, including Rijkaard spitting on Völler.

As the players walked off the pitch together, Rijkaard spat on Völler a second time. Early in the second half, Klinsmann fired the Germans ahead and Andreas Brehme curled home a second with eight minutes left. A Ronald Koeman penalty for the Netherlands in the 89th minute narrowed the score to 2-1 but the Germans saw the game out to gain some revenge for their exit to the Dutch in the previous European Championship.

Meanwhile, Cameroon v Colombia was goalless when Roger Milla was introduced as a second-half substitute, eventually breaking the deadlock midway through extra time. Three minutes later he netted a second after Colombia goalkeeper René Higuita was dispossessed by Milla while well out of his goal, leaving the striker free to slot the ball into the empty net. Though the deficit was soon reduced to 2-1, Cameroon held on to become the first African team to reach the World Cup quarter-finals. Costa Rica were beaten 4-1 by Czechoslovakia, for whom Tomáš Skuhravý scored the tournament's second and final hat-trick.

The Republic of Ireland's match with Romania remained goalless after extra time but the Irish won 5-4 on penalties. David O'Leary converted the penalty that clinched their place in the quarter-finals; they became the first team since Sweden in 1938 to reach the last eight in a World Cup finals without winning a match outright. Yugoslavia beat Spain 2-1 after extra time, with Dragan Stojković scoring both the Yugoslavs' goals. England were the final qualifier match against Belgium, midfielder David Platt's swivelling volley breaking the stalemate with the game moments away from a penalty shoot-out.

* * *

The first game of the quarter-finals saw Argentina and Yugoslavia, reduced to ten men after only half an hour, play out a goalless stalemate. The holders reached the semi-finals after winning the penalty shoot-out 3-2, despite Maradona having his kick saved. A second Argentine miss by Pedro Troglio looked to have eliminated them until goalkeeper Goycochea rescued his side by stopping the Yugoslavs' final two spot kicks.

The Republic of Ireland's run was brought to an end by a single goal from Schillaci in the first half of their quarter-final with Italy. West Germany beat Czechoslovakia with a 25th-minute Lothar Matthäus penalty.

England faced African opposition as they took on Cameroon in Naples on 1 July; it proved a very close-run thing for Bobby Robson and his team.

Senegal's squad at the 2022 World Cup, who faced England in the last 16 that year, was stacked with players of Premier League and European experience, including Chelsea's Édouard Mendy and Kalidou Koulibaly. In contrast, Cameroon's squad had 11 home-based players; pretty much amateur footballers. Five played top-level football abroad, all in France aside from the first-choice goalkeeper, Thomas N'Kono, signed by Espanyol after Cameroon's appearance in the 1982 World Cup, where a draw with the eventual winners Italy had signposted future heroics.

Milla was winding down his career with JS Saint-Pierroise but 1990 lent him a new lease of life. He told *The Guardian*, ' At 38 I couldn't have imagined I would play like that.' He did not score against England, instead acting as supplier for both of Cameroon's goals. After Platt's headed opener in the 25th minute, Milla was fouled by

Paul Gascoigne for Emmanuel Kundé to equalise from the penalty spot on the hour. Then, by controlling the ball with the sole of his boot and spinning within one movement, Milla found space to play in Eugène Ekéké to put Cameroon 2-1 up five minutes later.

'One of my great souvenirs is that we led England [until] seven minutes from the end of the game,' Milla said. A relaxed character off the field, for all his silky movement Milla played his best football when he was annoyed. 'He was angry at everything, angry at the opponent and angry about the referee,' said reserve goalkeeper Joseph-Antoine Bell. 'We finally discovered that he needed to be like that to deliver.'

The chaos of Cameroon's progress to the quarters via beating Argentina in the tournament's bruising opening match, delivering one of the greatest shocks of the World Cup finals, then Milla bagging two goals after René Higuita's disastrous attempt to play as a sweeper, had led England to seriously underestimate their opponents.

'A practical bye to the semi-finals' was the analysis attributed to Howard Wilkinson, then the Leeds manager, scouting in Italy for the English FA. Watching the game back, it appears Robson took 'Sgt Wilko' and such dismissiveness to heart. England only just prevailed in a match that very nearly escaped from them. 'Some fucking bye that,' a relieved and exhausted Chris Waddle told Wilkinson in the immediate aftermath.

Robson had also believed that England were not alone in carrying out a spying mission on the opposition. On the eve of the match, as Gary Lineker readied his usual penalty-taking routine, smashing the ball as hard as possible to the keeper's left in repeated tried and trusted fashion, he was warned by his manager that Cameroon had a spy operating in the Stadio San Paolo. Instead, Lineker took all of his practice kicks to the keeper's right, and Robson's suspicions, unfounded or not, would prove crucial.

'I knew I was going to put it to the keeper's left and, even as I hit it, I could see him going to his right,' Lineker said of the penalty he slotted past Thomas N'Kono to equalise for 2-2 seven minutes from time. 'At the end of normal time, Bobby hugged me and said, "I told you."'

Before that equaliser, England had ridden out a storm, 83 minutes with Gascoigne and Platt overrun in midfield and the attacking verve and improvisational attacking of Cameroon 'unbelievably smooth in their movements' as the BBC commentator Barry Davies put it. They were almost irresistible.

In the 2022 documentary *Green Lions: Cameroon '90*, John Barnes recalled, 'From an attacking perspective we had never come up against a team that attacked well from all angles of the pitch. We were defending and they were just so good coming forward. They gave us probably the hardest time of anyone. Even Germany did not give us that many problems. No one gave us that many problems.'

Substitute Eugène Ekéké, who had recently lost his mother, chipped the ball over Peter Shilton to give Cameroon a 2-1 lead on 65 minutes. He later remembered, 'When I score, my first thought is for her. She would have been so proud. And I wanted her to see that so badly.'

The Africans were just seven minutes away from the semi-finals and one of the greatest upsets in World Cup history. They should have tried to shut up shop and try to manage the game, but gave away a late free kick from which Mark Wright flicked it to Lineker who was hacked down inside the penalty area. In post-match interviews,

Lineker stated that as he placed the ball for the penalty he immediately thought of his brother, who was a very nervous watcher of his England games. Lineker also said he worried he would not be let back into the country if he missed the spot kick He knew from playing against N'kono for Barcelona that the goalkeeper tended to dive early at spot kicks, and he sent him the wrong way for the equaliser.

The game went to extra time, for England the second time in a row after their last-gasp win over Belgium. Gascoigne found Lineker running through again and the Spurs striker was brought down by N'Kono. Lineker blasted the penalty straight down the middle on 105 minutes. Despite some late pressure, England hung on to win 3-2.

Post-match, Lineker told ITV, 'It was very tough and they played very well and you've got to give them all the credit in the world. They've come underestimated into this World Cup but they've shown everybody that African football is very strong and I think we should applaud them.'

'At one time I thought we were on the plane home,' Bobby Robson admitted to ITV afterwards. 'We never underestimated Cameroon but they still surprised us through their speed, strength and running off the ball. We pulled it out of the fire and I don't really know how. I thought we showed a lot of spirit and a willingness to fight to the end. They were the better team when they went ahead but it was a see-sawing saga of a match and now we're in the world's top four in 1990 and I'm proud of our football for having achieved that.'

* * *

The first semi-final featured Italy and the world champions Argentina in Naples. Totò Schillaci scored yet again to put the hosts ahead in the 17th minute, but Claudio Caniggia equalised midway through the second half, breaking Walter Zenga's clean sheet streak throughout the tournament. There were no more goals in the 90 minutes or in extra time despite Maradona, who played for Naples in Serie A at the time, showing glimpses of magic, but there was a sending-off: Ricardo Giusti of Argentina was shown the red card in the 13th minute of extra time. Argentina went through on penalties, winning the shoot-out 4-3 after more heroics from Goycochea.

The other semi, between West Germany and England at the Stadio Delle Alpi, was goalless at half-time. Then, in the 60th minute, a free kick tapped to Andreas Brehme resulted in a shot that was deflected off Paul Parker into his own net. England equalised with ten minutes left through Lineker and it was 1-1 after 90 minutes. Extra time yielded more chances: Klinsmann was guilty of two glaring misses and both sides struck a post. England had another Platt goal disallowed for offside. The match went to penalties, and West Germany won it 4-3. The two matches had the exact same score at 1-1, an identical penalty shoot-out score at 4-3 and the same order of penalties scored.

Perhaps, given England's perceived lack of success, it's only natural to always look back to 1990. The wins over Cameroon and Belgium are remembered fondly because England did end up winning. The game against the Dutch is remembered fondly because England did end up going through. England did play very well against both the Netherlands and West Germany although they didn't win either encounter. There was far more to admire about England's general play in both 1986 and 1990, even in 1998, than the awful campaigns of 2010 and 2014.

For many England fans of a certain age, Italia 90 is the greatest World Cup they have lived through and the semi-final the greatest match. Shilton, Parker, Walker, Wright, Butcher, Pearce, Platt, Gascoigne, Waddle, Lineker, Beardsley. The 11 that started weren't all household names or supremely gifted individuals (with the exception of Paul Gascoigne). Goalkeeper Peter Shilton was 40, David Platt had never played competitive international football before the tournament, Gascoigne was a liability and there wasn't a defensive midfielder in sight.

Bobby Robson was under pressure even before the finals and was forced to announce that he would resign after England's run had concluded, regardless of how far they got. His contract was not renewed by the FA after eight years, and he would go on to coach Dutch club PSV after the World Cup. England went into the tournament with little expectation. A week before, they almost lost to Tunisia before drawing 1-1. The press savaged them and the squad responded with a media boycott. England qualified for the knockout stage, but it wasn't easy with those two draws against the Republic of Ireland and the Netherlands, and a 1-0 victory over Egypt, and only two goals in total. Inevitably, Gary Lineker was among the scorers, against Ireland. At the previous World Cup he had won the Golden Boot, and he ended up England's top scorer again, this time with four goals.

In that second match, England drew 0-0 against a Dutch team that included the magnificent Ruud Gullit, Marco van Basten and Frank Rijkaard. They outplayed the Dutch, with Gascoigne imperious. Bryan Robson injured his Achilles, which put him out of the tournament, but despite the loss of their captain the whole atmosphere changed. The team grew in confidence and the press became more supportive. There was now a sense of possibility.

The night before the semi-final, Bobby Robson called a meeting. Gary Lineker told *The Guardian*, 'Just before Bobby came in, I turned his clipboard over and wrote, "Even money he mentions the war." Then I turned it back over. So he walks in, stands up and says, "We beat them in the war!"' Like the rest of the squad, Lineker adored Robson, 'You'd run through a brick wall for him. He had a magnetic personality and was such an enthusiast, not just for football, for everything.' His meetings, though, 'could go on a bit. The one before the semi-final, we had to tell him, "We need to go out now, Bobby."'

Terry Butcher led England out that night. He told *The Guardian*, 'I cannot describe the pride and fear. Only Bobby Moore had been England captain in a World Cup semi-final before. You're treading in the steps of legends.'

In the eighth minute of extra time, Paul Gascoigne got booked. It meant he would miss the final if England got through, and resulted in one of the most famous images in footballing history, Gascoigne breaking down as his teammates tried to console him.

In the shoot-out, Lineker, Beardsley and Platt scored, as did Germany with their first three. Pearce, a regular penalty taker, ran up and smashed the ball straight at goalkeeper Bodo Illgner, who saved with his legs. The Germans scored their fourth, and it was down to Waddle to keep England in the tournament. He hit his penalty high into the stand, and West Germany became the first country to reach a third consecutive World Cup Final, where they beat Argentina 1-0.

Butcher recalled in *The Guardian*, 'The mood was very solemn. Back in the dressing room you were just numb. You go off for your shower, get dressed, go on the bus. You're like a zombie.'

'We were devastated,' said Mark Wright. 'You could hear a pin drop afterwards in the dressing room. Then Bobby said, "I'm proud of all of you." My grandmother used to say, "What's meant for you won't pass you by." And we just didn't have that extra little bit of fortune.'

It was only on their return to England that the squad realised they were regarded as heroes. 'What should have been a ten-minute journey from Luton airport to the hotel took a couple of hours,' Butcher recalled. 'There were hundreds of thousands of people lining the streets.

'When I saw all the people at the airport, the fans were singing our names and passing McDonald's and beer up to the bus. It was crazy. I've never known anything like it.'

The class of 1990 are unlike those who came before and after. They are not revered like the boys of 1966 who played for a pittance and won the World Cup. Nor are they like the 2000s golden generation, who earned big money and achieved so little. Butcher was substituted in the 71st minute of the semi-final. At the time, he hoped he had one more England game left in him: the final. But then reality hit home. He didn't play in the third/fourth play-off against Italy, which England lost 2-1.

He said, 'I knew I wasn't going to play for England again really. My knees were gone, and I was 31. I thought: my days are done here. I knew the semi-final was my last game, as it was for a good number of the boys.' Yes, they were proud of what they had achieved, but they'd hoped for so much more. 'We'd made amends for 86 and the hand of God,' Butcher said. 'We'd gone far, but we hadn't gone far enough.'

* * *

The third/fourth play-off saw three goals in a 15-minute spell near the end of the match. Roberto Baggio opened the scoring after a mistake by Peter Shilton, in his 125th and final game before international retirement, presented a simple opportunity. A header by David Platt levelled ten minutes later but Schillaci was fouled in the penalty area with four minutes to play, leading to a penalty. Schillaci himself got up to convert the kick to win him the tournament's Golden Boot for his six-goal tally. Nicola Berti had a goal ruled out minutes later, but the hosts claimed third place with a 2-1 victory.

* * *

The 1990 final is often cited as one of the most cynical and ugliest World Cup Finals. It was a bad-tempered game, notable for the first two red cards in the tournament's showpiece match. Football blogger Ian Morrison wrote in a 2020 piece titled 'World in Motion, the 1990 World Cup', 'The game did little for football but there was one consolation: had the Argentines lifted the World Cup with two wins and five goals in their seven matches it would have been a catastrophe for the game. At least their awful approach to Italia 90 had gone unrewarded.'

West Germany attacked from the beginning of the match, with Rudi Völler going close early on following a free kick by Brehme, but he fired wide. They soon won another free kick in a more dangerous position when Pierre Littbarski was fouled just outside the box. Brehme's shot hit the wall and Klaus Augenthaler's long-range follow-up strike was saved by Sergio Goycochea. Soon after, Völler's header and Littbarski's curling shot went high and wide. In the 13th minute Brehme's outswinging cross appeared to strike the arm of defender Oscar Ruggeri but the Mexican referee Edgardo Codesal waved away any German appeals for a penalty.

Five minutes later, Völler was brought down in the area, but Codesal waved play on. German captain Lothar Matthäus's cross found Völler but his header was wide of the target. In the 38th minute, Argentina won a dangerous free kick when José Basualdo was fouled by Guido Buchwald. Diego Maradona's effort went up and over the wall but flew over the bar.

At half-time it was goalless but the Germans had a few chances at the start of the second half. Littbarski cut inside, dribbled past three defenders, but his shot from outside the box went just wide. Then Thomas Berthold and Völler failed to capitalise from dangerous free kicks taken by Brehme. In the 58th minute, Goycochea appeared to take down Klaus Augenthaler inside the penalty area, but Codesal again refused to award a penalty kick.

In the 65th minute, Pedro Monzón – only on as a substitute at half-time – became the first player to be sent off at a FIFA World Cup Final, after being shown a straight red card for a reckless, studs-up challenge on Klinsmann. The German dived again on the ground, making a meal of the tackle, but later claimed that the tackle left a large gash on his shin. On 78 minutes Matthäus lost the ball inside his own penalty area and then appeared to trip Gabriel Calderón but Codesal once again waved to play on, amid loud penalty appeals from the Argentinian players.

Six minutes from time, Codesal awarded a penalty for Roberto Sensini's sliding tackle on Völler. Regular taker

Matthäus had been forced to replace his boots during the match and did not feel comfortable in the new ones, so Brehme took the kick and scored into the corner, even though Goycochea had dived the right way.

In the 87th minute, Gustavo Dezotti received a straight red card for having hauled down Jürgen Kohler when he grabbed the defender's neck after he refused to give up the ball in an attempt to waste time. After dismissing Dezotti, Codesal was surrounded and jostled by the rest of the Argentinian team, with Maradona receiving a yellow card for dissent. There was no more scoring and West Germany were 1-0 winners.

In total, West Germany had 16 shots on target. German coach Franz Beckenbauer said later, 'There were no doubts whatsoever who was going to win. For 90 minutes we attacked Argentina and there was no feeling of any danger that a goal would be scored against us. As I saw it, we outplayed them from beginning to end.' Beckenbauer said that the penalty 'was not the key to the game because in any case we would have scored, even if it had taken extra time; 1-0 by a penalty doesn't give a fair idea of this game. We could have won, 3-0. I don't remember a single chance Argentina had to score a goal.'

Argentina only had one shot on goal. Without four players who'd been suspended, suspended including striker Claudio Caniggia, they focused on defending at all costs, hoping for a penalty shoot-out. At the time, the 1990 final was the lowest-scoring final in the history of the competition, although this record was broken four years later when Brazil beat Italy on penalties after 120 goalless minutes. The 1990 victory gave West Germany their third World Cup, also making them the team to have played in the most finals at the time with three wins and three defeats, as well as avenging their defeat at the hands of Argentina in the previous final.

It also meant that Beckenbauer became the only person to have been a runner-up and a winner in the final as a player (1966 and 1974 respectively) and as a coach (1986, 1990). Added to that, he also won a bronze medal as a player in 1970. Having won on penalties against England in the semi-finals, West Germany became the first team to have won by that method en route to the title. This was repeated four years later by Brazil, France in 1998, Italy in 2006 and Argentina, who won two shoot-outs in 2022, including the final.

With their third title, West Germany – in their final tournament before national reunification – became the most successful World Cup nation at the time along with Italy and Brazil, who had also won three titles each at that time. Franz Beckenbauer became the first man to both captain, in 1974, and manage a World Cup-winning team, and only the second man – after Mário Zagallo of Brazil – to win the World Cup as a player and then as a manager. It was also the first time that a team from UEFA had won the final against a non-European team.

Maybe it wasn't the best World Cup you will ever see. Not many Brazilians or Dutch will reflect with much fondness. The statistics are not positive: the fewest goals per game in the competition's history and the most red cards at that point. If anyone wants to squabble about that, they could do worse than gawp at Roberto Baggio's salsa through the Czechoslovakia defence and Dragan Stojković's masterpiece against Spain, listen to 'World in Motion', marvel at the reaction to François Omam-Biyik's opening-day goal and the madness of Benjamin Massing's tackle to mow down a galloping Claudio Caniggia in the Miracle of Milan.

Much of that was to do with the venue, Italy, where *calcio* is a religion. At the time, Serie A was the best league in the world by a distance, and the game has rarely felt as important as it did around then. Two days after the final, Ian Ridley wrote in *The Guardian*, 'Probably only in Italy could such an unsatisfying tournament overall, in footballing terms, that is, have been such a success.'

On the field, Italia 90 had two major things going for it: an almost ceaseless supply of drama, and several individual and collective stories that went straight into World Cup folklore. It's fitting that such a dramatic tournament should have set a new record of four penalty shoot-outs – including, uniquely, two in the semi-finals – that has not been bettered (though there were also four in 2006). Some felt those semi-finals were cheapened by the manner in which they were decided, but both were immense matches regardless – probably the best pair of semis in any World Cup, which counterbalances the appalling final.

The Republic of Ireland sneaked into the quarter-finals in their first World Cup. There was the thuggery and brilliance of Cameroon, the first African side to reach the quarter-finals. Gary Lineker's nervelessness from the spot against Cameroon, particularly as, in the first instance, he was taking England's first penalty for four years. Careca's two superb goals against Sweden. Ruud Gullit's stunning goal against Ireland and Belgium's outstanding display with ten men against Uruguay.

It might not have been a World Cup of great games, but it was one of memorable tales and epic emotions: Roger Milla shook his 38-year-old hips at the corner flag for himself, and for Africa. Totò Schillaci smashed in shots, wheeled off with his crazed eyes virtually popping out of their sockets and became an unlikely hero. Frank Rijkaard and Rudi Völler were entwined in a spitting red card shocker. David O'Leary kept his legs from buckling to score a legendary knockout penalty.

Four countries no longer exist in the way they did then. It was the last World Cup in which West Germany competed (unification came later in 1990), then Yugoslavia began to break up in 1991, and Czechoslovakia split in 1992. This tournament represented the last appearance at a major finals of the Soviet Union team, as by the time the next European Championship came around their place was taken up by the CIS, which was effectively just Russia.

Sunday, 24 June saw two epic games in the second round. One of Brazil and Argentina were going out, and one of the Netherlands and West Germany, but to lose to their most hated rivals was utterly unthinkable. Brazil lost to Argentina in one of the greatest smash-and-grabs of all, with Diego Maradona producing one of the great assists to win the match, while the Netherlands were beaten 2-1 by West Germany in Milan. It had been a very unhappy tournament for the Dutch, who spent the tournament fighting in their camp. The Netherlands had finished up playing the Germans after drawing lots with the Republic of Ireland, who had the easier task of facing Romania.

West Germany, who had lost the previous two finals, were one of many tales of the summer. They were as good a power team as there has ever been, with scarcely a weakness and with world-class players in Andreas Brehme, Lothar Matthäus, Jürgen Klinsmann and Rudi Völler. They were worthy champions after beating Yugoslavia, the Netherlands, Czechoslovakia, England and Argentina.

England's journey was equally compelling, from 'No Football Please, We're English' (the headline in *Gazzetta dello Sport* after the appalling first match against Ireland) to a performance of genuine continental sophistication in that semi-final against West Germany. Their progress was fortunate: a three-goal win would not have flattered Cameroon in the quarter-final, and Belgium had slightly the better of an excellent second-round game but, by using a European sweeper system in a country of 4-4-2, they came so close to reaching the final.

Italia 90 saw Klinsmann producing an outstanding individual performance against the Netherlands, along with West Germany's outstanding left-back Brehme; the skilful and exciting Yugoslavia team, so impressive in beating Spain; Roberto Baggio's brilliant solo goal; the seemingly impenetrable Italian defence, which went a World Cup record 517 minutes before conceding; Maradona at his Naples home in the semi-final and his superb penalty in the shoot-out that sent Italy into despair.

The most one-sided World Cup Final in recent memory was fittingly won by a penalty, taken by Brehme, as regular taker Matthäus was wearing new boots. It was a World Cup of iconic kits too: West Germany, Colombia, Cameroon, Yugoslavia, England and Italy all played in striking shirts. The 1990 World Cup was an unforgettable summer of highs and lows, agony and ecstasy, triumph and despair. Scotland were there on the world stage as part of the drama, close once again to the promised land of the knockout stages.

Bibliography

Bleasdale, J., *Scotland's Swedish Adventure* (Pitch Publishing, 2022)

Brogan, T., *Scotland 101* (Pitch Publishing, 2023)

Brogan, T., *We Made Them Angry: Scotland at the 1982 World Cup* (Pitch Publishing, 2022)

Brown, C., *The Game of My Life* (Blake Publishing, 2011)

Dalglish, K. & Winter, H., *My Autobiography* (Hodder Paperbacks, 1997)

Davis, P., *All Played Out: The Full Story of Italia 90* (Yellow Jersey, 1998)

Davis, P., *One Night In Turin* (Yellow Jersey, 2010)

Ferguson, A., *Managing My Life* (Hodder & Stoughton, 2000)

Gordon, R., *Scotland 74: A World Cup Story* (Black and White Publishing, 2014)

Grech, P., *Echoes of An Italian Summer: Stories from Italia 90* (Pitch Publishing, 2023)

Hart, S., *World In Motion: The Story of Italia 90* (Mount Vernon Publishing, 2024)

Keir, R., *Scotland The Complete International Football Record* (Breedon Books, 2001)

Leatherdale, C., *Scotland's Quest for World Cup* (Desert Island Books, 1994)

Leighton, J & Robertson, K., *In The Firing Line* (Mainstream Publishing, 2000)

MacLeod, A., *The Ally MacLeod Story* (Stanley Paul, 1979)

Macpherson, A., *Adventures in the Golden Age – Scotland at the World Cup Finals 1974–1998* (Black and White Publishing, 2018)

McCall, S., *Stuart McCall's Own Story* (Mainstream Publishing, 1998)

McCoist, A. & Brankin, C., *My Story* (Mainstream Publishing, 1992)

McColl, G., *78: How Scotland Lost the World Cup* (Headline, 2006)

McColl, G., *Scotland in the World Cup Finals* (Andre Deutsch, 1998)

McPherson, D., *A Tale Of Two Cities* (Mainstream Publishing, 1996)

Potter, D., *Wizards and Bravehearts: History of the Scotland Side* (Tempus, 2004)

Smith, P., *Scotland Players Who's Who, 1872–2013* (Pitch Publishing, 2013)

Souness, G. & Harris, B., *No Half Measures* (Harper Collins, 1987)

Tait, J., *Scotland at 150* (Jicks Publishing, 2023)

Ward, A., *Scotland The Team* (Breedon Books, 1987)

Newspapers
Daily Record
Glasgow Evening Times
The Scotsman
The Herald
The Daily Mail
The Guardian
Evening Telegraph Courier
Liverpool Echo

Magazines
World Soccer
Football Monthly
Inside Football
World Cup 90
Shoot
Match

Websites
bbc.co.uk/football
RSSSF Scotland International Results
londonhearts.com/scotland/scotland.htm
scottishfa.co.uk
footballia.eu/teams/scotland
italia1990.com
dailyrecord.co.uk/sport/football/
theguardian.com/football
dailymail.co.uk/sport/football/index.html
liverpoolecho.co.uk/sport/football

Match programmes

1986 Scotland v Bulgaria

1986 Scotland v Luxembourg

1987 Scotland v England

1987 Scotland v Brazil

1987 Scotland v Hungary

1987 Scotland v Belgium

1988 Scotland v Colombia

1988 Scotland v England

1988 Scotland v Yugoslavia

1989 Scotland v France

1989 Scotland v Cyprus

1989 Scotland v England

1989 Scotland v Chile

1989 Scotland v Norway

1990 Scotland v Argentina

1990 Scotland v East Germany

1990 Scotland v Egypt

1990 Scotland v Poland

1990 Scotland v Romania

1990 Scotland v Switzerland

1991 Scotland v USSR

1991 Scotland v Bulgaria

1991 Scotland v San Marino

Videos

Scotland World Cup Story 1990

1990 World Cup Highlights

Scotland Official History 1992

Scotland Euro 92 A Tribute

YouTube
BBC Review 1990 World Cup
ITV Review 1990 World Cup
All The Goals 1990 World Cup
The Squad: Scotland Euro 92 Story
Faith, Hope and Calamity, 1994
Scotland's Game, BBC 2016